MAGELLAN

OVERLEAF
LEFT The Virgin of the Navigators
to whom sailors prayed for protection from
the dangers of the sea.
RIGHT A tin-glazed earthenware
bowl showing the Arms of Portugal. It was
made in Valencia during the first half of the
fifteenth century.
ENDPAPERS
A romantic sixteenth-century engraving
of a Spanish armada

STRENVI HISPANIAE NAVIGANTES REGINA MARIS
ARDENTISSIME FLVCTVVM VENTORVMQVE
PERICVLA SVSTINVERVNT

IN PERICVLIS MARIS
ESTO NOBIS PROTECTIO

MAGELLAN
And the First Circumnavigation of the World
Ian Cameron

Saturday Review Press
New York

Designed and produced for
George Weidenfeld and Nicolson Limited
London

*Filmset and printed Offset Litho in
Great Britain by*
Cox & Wyman Ltd,
London, Fakenham and Reading

ISBN 0–8415–0257–9
Library of Congress number 73–75734

Saturday Review Press
*380 Madison Avenue
New York, New York 10017*

Contents

Introduction

TODAY, WHEN ALL THE EARTH IS SO WELL KNOWN, it is difficult to appreciate the problems which faced sixteenth-century explorers. Ferdinand Magellan was one of them, and it is astonishing to realise that in his day even the existence of the Pacific Ocean was undreamt of, for the Earth itself was thought to be much smaller than was finally proved.

As a young man Magellan had taken part in a number of maritime Portuguese forays in the Far East, and had sailed into Indonesian and Philippine waters in search of the much coveted Spice Islands. This book, however, is mainly concerned with the great voyage which made his name when, sailing *westward* in the service of King Charles of Spain, he at last found *el paso*, the narrow strait through the tip of South America which now bears his name, and proved to be the gateway to the ocean which he called *Mar Pacifico*. Sailing across under the most terrible conditions, he finally arrived at the Philippine Islands. Thus it can be claimed that he was the first man to 'circum-navigate' the world.

Magellan is a name known to every child, but the nature of his achievement is seldom appreciated. With small, unmanageable ships, completely at the mercy of capricious winds, his voyage included 25,000 miles across completely unknown seas. Faced with sick and mutinous crews, with constant anxiety about food and water and the repeated ravages of scurvy, only his personal drive and determination brought his often unwilling armada to its destination.

Before he ever set out, conflicting councils, jealous rivalries and the planned undermining of his authority presented almost insuperable problems. Perhaps it is the natural fate of great proposals to be denigrated, both by those with vested interests and those of faint heart and little imagination. However that may be, Magellan showed great strength of character and tenacity of purpose in dealing with his enemies, both at home and at sea.

History relates graphically the cruelty and destruction wrought by so many voyagers of his day, but historians should be careful in their criticism, arising from a later culture, of what was then accepted behaviour. Yet Magellan, ruthless in compelling his men towards the attainment of his objectives, showed great compassion for his sick, and unusual tolerance and understanding in dealing with the native peoples he encountered. The only time when he appears to have departed from this attitude led him to his death. So much does his behaviour on that occasion seem out of keeping with his nature, that one may suspect the reports on which the story is based – especially since all his personal papers and records were destroyed by his detractors. As the author points out, thus was he deprived of his rightful place in history.

Magellan emerges as a man of great power, exceptional determination and total dedication to the tasks he undertook. In him was the imaginative spark which drove him to discovery. These characteristics, combined with his skilled seamanship, led to one of the greatest exploratory journeys of all time.

V. E. Fuchs

Prologue

THE TIME WAS A LITTLE BEFORE SUNSET on an evening in October 1516 (the exact date is not known); the place was a courtyard in the royal palace on the bank of the Tagus, where Dom Manuel the Fortunate, King of Portugal, was enthroned in state on his dais of ebony and gold. All day a succession of supplicants had been kneeling at the King's feet, humbly begging in public those favours for which they lacked the influence to petition in private. By the time a herald was announcing the name of the last petitioner the sun was setting and the King was tired.

'Fernão de Magalhães!'

A murmur of surprise ran through the court. For Ferdinand Magellan was a person of substance, an officer (albeit a junior one) of the royal household, and certainly not the sort of man one would expect to go down on his knees in public. Heads craned forward as the short, thickset figure limped awkwardly to the dais. And Dom Manuel frowned; he had disliked Magellan when as boys they had served together as pages in his aunt's Court; the years had done nothing to mellow his feelings.

In a low voice the mariner began his petition. He outlined his nine years of service in Africa, India and Indonesia, mentioning the great battles in which he had fought and the three times he had been seriously wounded; he ended with a plea that he might be granted the extra few pence a month which would signify a rise in rank to *fidalgo da casa de El Rei*. Dom Manuel refused. Magellan had half expected this, and he stayed on his knees. He was making another petition now: that he might be given command of one of the royal caravels soon to set sail for the Moluccas, the fabulous Spice Islands of the East. Again Dom Manuel refused; he had, he said curtly, no use for Magellan's services either in a caravel or anywhere else. Magellan had not expected this; his sense of justice was outraged, and his indignation was all the greater because his humiliation was in open court. 'Then may I be permitted', he cried, 'to seek service under another Lord?'

Dom Manuel rose from his throne, his commanding figure towering majestically over the insignificant Magellan. 'Serve whom you will, Clubfoot', he said loudly. 'It is a matter of indifference to us.'

For a moment Magellan did not move; not in his worst nightmare had he imagined anything so terrible as this; then, automatically, he bent forward to kiss the King's hand, a ritual traditionally performed by loyal *fidalgos* at the end of their audience. But Dom Manuel put his hands behind his back.

As Magellan, humiliated for the second time, backed haltingly from the royal presence, his limp hampered him; he lost his balance and almost fell.

'Don't trip over your cloven hoof!' an usher shouted, and a ripple of laughter ran round the court.

Half blind with anger and grief, Magellan stumbled from the palace.

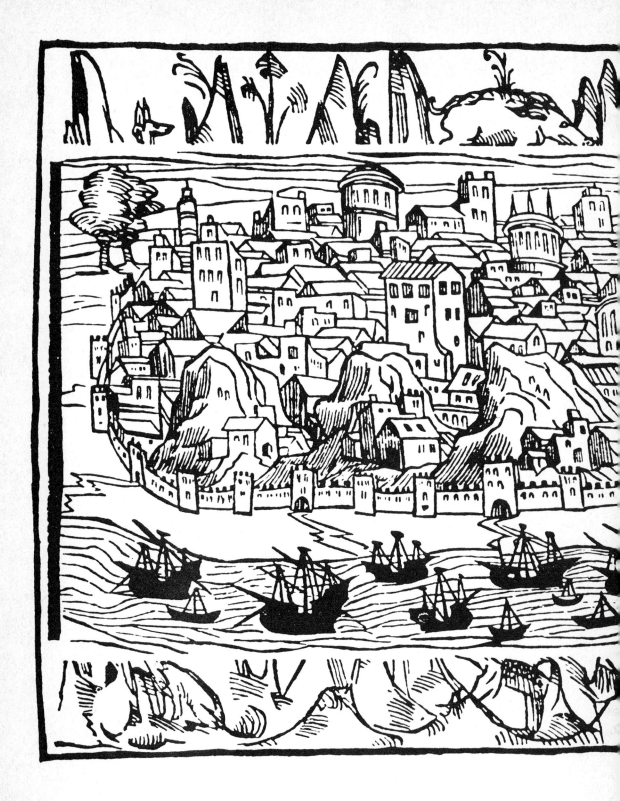

1 The Apprentice

MAGELLAN WAS BORN in the spring of 1480 – again the exact date is not known – third child of Dom Roy and Donha Alda Magalhães. His father was one of the petty nobility of the northern province of Minho, being descended, somewhat dubiously, from a cadet branch of the de Sousas. He was brought up in the Torre de Magalhães, a farmhouse which had taken gradual shape, each generation making an addition here or there, round the foundations of an eleventh-century watch-tower. This farmhouse was rambling and unpretentious; the cattle, goats and poultry occupied the lower floor, the Magellan family the upper. This fact is of some significance. In sixteenth-century Portugal a man's life was shaped very largely by the circumstances of his birth; Magellan's admirers, both then and now, have often described him as 'one of the nobility', whereas his detractors have dubbed him 'a peasant-farmer'; the truth lies halfway in between.

At the age of seven, Ferdinand was sent to school in the near-by monastery of Vila nova de Mura; here he learned his cate-chism and the rudiments of arithmetic and Latin. Since in later life his achievements were practical and physical rather than theoretical and mental, it seems that the open-air life of the farm played a greater part in shaping his character than the academic atmosphere of the cloisters. Be that as it may, his childhood was a happy one: a united family living a comfortable, uncompli-cated life amid surroundings as beautiful as any in western Europe.

The early sixteenth century, however, was the age of the Renaissance. Boys of spirit were not likely to remain contentedly at home when the whole world with its expanding horizons was beckoning them. And at the age of twelve Ferdinand was apprenticed as a page to Queen Leonora's Court.

Queen Leonora's School for Pages was a microcosm of Renaissance Portugal, mirroring with faithful precision the country's rigid social hierarchy, its family feuds, its nepotism, its boundless energy and above all its love-hate relationship with the sea. The school was attached to the Queen's Court rather than the King's because the King was under constant threat of assassination, and his Court consisted of little more than a per-petually-shifting camp. The Queen's Court, on the other hand, should in theory have been relatively stable, since it was based on Lisbon; in practice, however, it too proved largely peripa-tetic, the whole conglomeration of courtiers, officials and

PREVIOUS PAGES
Sixteenth-century Lisbon where Magellan served his apprenticeship as a page. This woodcut is from the *Libro de Grande-zas y Cosas Memorables de Espana*, produced in Seville in 1548.

BELOW King John II of Portugal who continued to sponsor the maritime pro-gramme which his great-uncle, Henry the Navigator, began. It was under his auspices that Magellan studied cartography, astronomy and celestial navigation.

hangers-on moving round the country from castle to castle and monastery to monastery in an effort to avoid the plague. The main items in the pages' curriculum were music, dancing, Court etiquette, hunting, jousting and swordsmanship. These subjects would have been studied at any Court in Europe. Queen Leonora's pages, however, were unique in that they were also expected to achieve proficiency in cartography, astronomy and celestial navigation – a range of activities which indicates very clearly the maritime orientation of the Portuguese Court. The pages were supervised by Duke Manuel, the brother-in-law and rival of the King. Duke Manuel was handsome, able and the centre of Lisbon's *dolce vita*, but he was no friend of Magellan's. To quote C. M. Parr in his biography *So Noble A Captain*:

Duke Manuel took a dislike to Ferdinand from the start. Whether his unfriendliness was caused by some prank of the young page, was based on political factionalism, or was a simple case of incompatible personalities, is not known; but the existence of an enduring grudge is affirmed by contemporary historians.

'Duke Manuel took a dislike to Ferdinand from the start'

In spite of the Duke's hostility, Ferdinand's early years as a page seem to have been happy enough, and he must have had high hopes of advancement in the maritime service of the King. This was the decade of Columbus's discoveries in the West Indies, and Magellan, like most of the youngsters at Court, must have longed for the day when he too would be at sea with a chance to 'roll back the frontiers of the world'. When he was fifteen, however, he was overtaken by the first of the calamities which were, time and again, to blight his career. King John of Portugal was assassinated, and Duke Manuel succeeded to the throne.

It is difficult today to appreciate just how heavy a blow this must have been for Magellan. King John had led a progressive maritime faction; Duke Manuel led a conservative agricultural one. The succession therefore brought about a fundamental change in policy. Those, like the Magellan family, who had favoured overseas commitments were swept from office; their places were taken by supporters of the new regime, and Ferdinand found himself overnight a would-be mariner with little prospect of a ship. He must have despaired at first of his future. He was, however, too insignificant a pawn on the political board to lose office; he continued his training as a page, albeit now with little prospect of patronage or advancement.

ABOVE Battles between Arabs, who were protecting their monopoly, and the invading Portuguese, eager to set up trading compounds, were frequent. Magellan took part in many such encounters during the early part of his career. This particular battle was at Surat in Gujurat, north of Bombay.

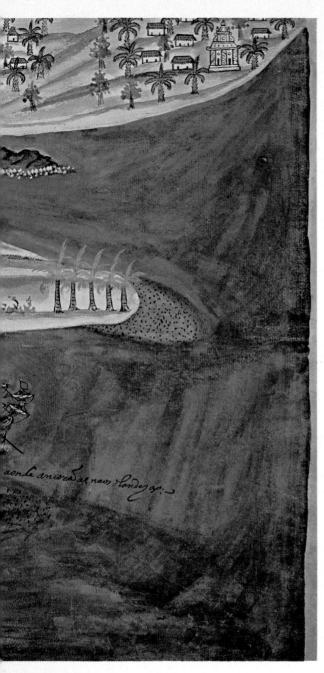

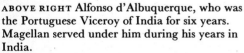

DOFRACISCODA
LMEIDA·VISOREI·

ABOVE RIGHT Alfonso d'Albuquerque, who was
the Portuguese Viceroy of India for six years.
Magellan served under him during his years in
India.

RIGHT Dom Francisco de Almeida, first Viceroy of
India. During much of his term of office he was
involved in combat, establishing the Portuguese
along the Malabar Coast. He was killed in a fight
with the Hottentots on the site of present-day
Cape Town in 1510.

For several years King Manuel turned his back on the sea; the Jews (the *entrepreneurs* of trade) were expelled, and the Knights of Christ (the traditional aristocracy) were promoted to high office in Church and State. However, one of the few maritime ventures which the King did authorise was to prove unexpectedly successful. In the last year of the century Vasco da Gama discovered the sea route to India, and Dom Manuel was suddenly able to reap the harvest which his predecessors had so laboriously sowed. In his own words:

We learn that our captains really *did* discover India the Great and other kingdoms that border it: that they sailed up the coast, finding rivers, buildings and large cities, as well as a great population much

C. de Gel

A Theodore de Bry engraving of a Portuguese armada departing from Lisbon. It was in such an armada that in 1503 Magellan set sail for service in the East on an expedition of conquest led by the Viceroy of India, Francisco de Almeida.

occupied in trading in spices and precious jewels, which are forwarded first to Mecca and then to Cairo, from which city they are distributed throughout the world. We hope, with God's help, that all this great trade shall from henceforth be diverted to the people and ships of our kingdom.

Magellan was nineteen when Vasco da Gama returned in triumph from the East with his splendid cargo of spice from the Moluccas, silk and jade from China, narcotics and dyes from the Gulf of Cambay, 'emeralds and pearls from Tabrobane, and sealed virgins from the land of Kilwa'. It had been an epic voyage, and one which was to inaugurate a new phase in Portuguese history, for this hitherto impoverished nation became quite suddenly, one of the wealthiest in Europe. After half a century of largely profitless exploration the riches of the Orient came flooding into her ports; she became overnight the emporium of Europe, and although her new-found wealth was not always used to the best advantage, it brought none the less a magnificent show of opulence. Shipyards and docks sprang up on either bank of the Tagus, palaces and mansions mushroomed at every port, the women (and the men) took to wearing costly silks, exotic furs and jewels more precious than were dreamed of in the Courts of Florence and Rome; it became fashionable to copy the Eastern style of architecture, to employ Hindu slaves as servants and to serve Indian curries at table. And though it is true that the effort bled her white and cost her a tenth of her population – that is to say more than half of her young, able-bodied men – yet her moment of glory was none the less as splendid as it was transient.

For Magellan, the excitement of the first years of this new century was tempered by personal frustration. As C. M. Parr relates in *So Noble a Captain*:

Everyone at court now wanted to sail to India to make his fortune, and Magellan was no exception. However it required political influence to be allowed to enlist in one of the expeditions, and this he lacked. Instead he was forced to work hard in fitting out ships for the fortunate few to sail in. He must have eaten his heart out as year after year a returning fleet discharged its home-coming adventurers covered with nautical distinction and laden with material gains.

However in 1504, King Manuel appointed Francisco d'Almeida Viceroy of India with orders to proceed to the East on an expedition of conquest; and at last Magellan was given his long-awaited opportunity. He obtained leave from his appointment at Court and enlisted as a seaman. So, six frustrating year after Vasco da Gama's famous homecoming and a few weeks after his own twenty-fifth birthday, Magellan, together with his brother Diogo, and his cousin Francisco Serrano, set sail for service in the East.

He was to spend eight years in the East. He went out a callow *sobresaliente* (supernumerary), serving without pay, and sharing accommodation with the crew. He returned an experienced sea captain; a veteran of many desperate land and sea battles, who

RIGHT A romantic
representation of the caravel,
from the *Libre de cololat
tractat dels fets maritims* of 1502.
LEFT These diagrams show
the flexibility of the caravels'
rigging. The lateen rig was
considered more useful for
inshore reconnaissance and
coastal trading, while the
square rig proved more
suitable for long passages in
conditions of stable wind.

had been wounded twice and had won and lost at least two
fortunes; a man too who had not only commanded his own
caravel but had taken her on a secret voyage 'beyond the sunrise
and the Isles of Spice into seas no Christian man as yet had
entered into'. These were his formative years, the years in which
he found his vocation.

The fleet in which Magellan sailed was commanded by Dom
Francisco de Almeida and was the largest ever to leave Portugal
– twenty-two ships and 1,980 men – for its objective was not
only to trade but also to set up a chain of fortified bases along
the coast of Africa. As the vessels weighed anchor, the waterfront was thronged by a silent concourse of relatives and friends;
silent because on almost any expedition to the East there was a

crew loss of fifty per cent, and for this particular expedition the astrologers had cast an unfavourable horoscope. The vessels themselves, in contrast, were gay with flags and song. We do not know which ship Magellan was embarked in, but it was probably one of the smaller caravels.

A caravel was to be his home, waking and sleeping, for most of the remainder of his life; so a description of one of these remarkable vessels will help us to visualise his surroundings.

If a list were made of the most efficient ships in history, the Portuguese caravel would vie for first place with the Viking longship and the Phoenician trader. The special distinction of the caravel was that it could sail against the wind. Never before in the Western world had a vessel enjoyed this facility, with the consequence that for more than a thousand years shipping had been pinned to the coast of Europe by the prevailing westerly winds. The caravel broke this stalemate by making use of a revolutionary type of sail, a lateen or triangular sail of the type used by an Arab dhow. Arab dhows have a unique capacity for sailing against the wind – this is their *raison d'être*, for they are obliged to cross and recross the Indian Ocean from east to west and back again during the same fair-weather monsoon. The rig which enables them to do this is described by a contemporary chronicler:

> The dhow's yardarm is not fixed at right-angles to the mast, but is hung from it obliquely. Its sail is triangular, with the lower edge almost feathering the sea. The yards are rigged from the deck, and by simply moving them from one side of the vessel to the other, the sail will open from any quarter according to the direction of the wind. Thus all winds are favourable to the dhow; and even with a breeze from the side she will sail as well as though it were from astern.

This rig was introduced into the Mediterranean in the early fifteenth century, and it brought a new flexibility to Western seamanship. Sailing ability alone, however, does not make a good vessel; the necessary seaworthiness was achieved in the caravel by grafting the Eastern lateen sail on to an eminently suitable Western hull.

You can see them today at the mouth of the Tagus, Douro or Mondego: broad-beamed, shallow-draught *frigata* (wine boats) riding the swell as comfortably as any vessel of their size on earth. The peculiarity of these vessels is that they are built of flush-fitting timbers as opposed to overlapping ones – indeed the

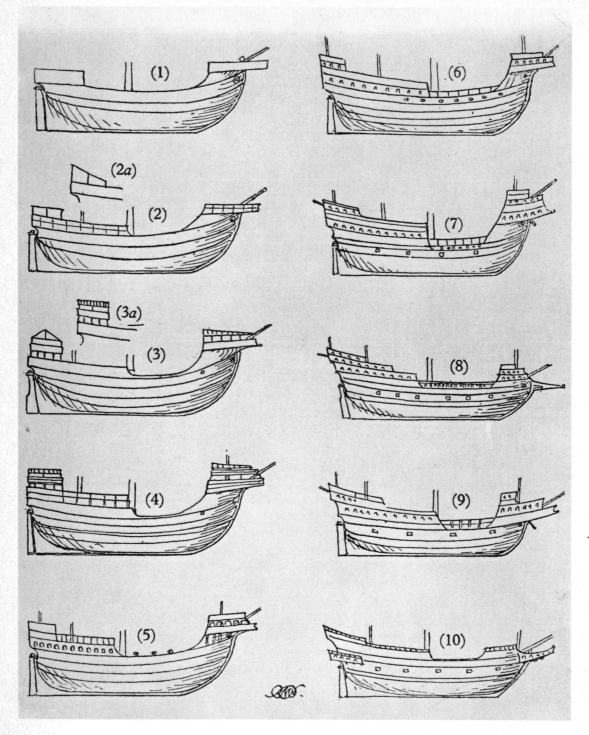

There was a considerable change in the hull construction of purpose-built merchant ships between 1400 and 1600. Diagrams 6 and 7 show the characteristic high fo'c'sle of the carrack type; 8, 9 and 10 show the development of the galleon with its finer lines and characteristic beakhead.

The evolution of sail plan, 1430 to 1600. Diagrams 1 shows a primitive
late medieval cog; 2, 3 and 4 show stages in development of merchantmen
of the carrack type; 5 and 6 are sixteenth-century galleons.

word caravel has passed into English use as 'carvel', a shipbuilding term which denotes a hull constructed in this particular way. In the second decade of the fifteenth century an unknown Tagus shipwright hit on the idea of axling his *frigata*'s rudder in the manner of a Baltic cog; in the third decade another shipwright added the lateen sail. The result was the caravel, a brilliant composite, adapting local methods of hull design to the rig of the East and the rudder of the North.

These vessels were the work-horses of the Portuguese explorers. Without them there would have been no golden age of discovery, and no circumnavigation of the world.

Magnificent sailing ships as the caravels undoubtedly were, when Magellan embarked that spring his first impression must have been of frailty, squalor and almost unbelievable overcrowding. Here are some basic facts about the ship in which he was about to sail. Her length would have been roughly seventy-five feet from stem to stern, her beam twenty-six feet, her

A reconstruction of a Portuguese square-rigged caravel of the late fifteenth century. These vessels were the work-horses of the Portuguese and Spanish explorers.

draught seven feet and her weight a shade under a hundred tons; this makes her barely a quarter the size of a fourth-century Phoenician trader. In theory she would have had two decks, but in practice her lower deck seems to have been broken by so large a hatch that it consisted of little more than a shelf round the interior of the hull; on this were mounted the carronades (which could be fired only in fine weather). Her hold was six feet deep and never empty of bilgewater. Since her toilet facilities consisted of no more than a stern-slung cage which could not be reached in bad weather, her crew had no option but to make frequent use of the bilge, which, when stirred up in heavy seas, gave off a stench so overpowering that it made even the hardened seamen vomit. At night, cockroaches and rats climbed out of the sediment and came swarming into every part of the ship. Each man was allowed to bring aboard only a small sea-chest and a roll of bedding; these had to be stowed on the open waist-deck: a damp, windswept and overcrowded square on

This reconstruction, also of the late fifteenth century, shows the caravel lateen-rigged. These ships were carvel-built, two-masted, or later three-masted, and had only one deck, usually completely open.

which were crammed the better part of a hundred men. Yet it was the life Magellan yearned for and, what is more, the life he clove to of his own free will for the rest of his days.

Magellan's first weeks at sea foreshadowed none of the excitements to come: fair winds, moderate seas and shore-leave at Tenerife and the Cape Verdes. As the armada neared the approaches to the Cape of Good Hope, however, the temperature dropped, the seas rose, the schools of flying fish were superseded by schools of whales, and ice began to form on the caravels' rigging. Almeida was leading his vessels far to the south in an effort to pick up the wind-belt of the roaring forties: sound navigation, but hard on the crew, for it was winter in this Southern Hemisphere, and when they did at last pick up the forties they were appalled by the ferocity of wind and wave. For week after week a full-blown gale, laced with sleet, tore through their rigging with such fury that it ripped even the storm canvas to shreds, while enormous waves, shrouded in mist and snow, came surging in endless succession out of the west, each, as it towered over the caravels' stern, threatening to engulf them.

In Magellan's vessel the boatswain was unable for a fortnight to light a fire, and the crew had nothing hot either to eat or to drink. They clawed round the Cape on the shortest day of the year, 21 June, and altered course thankfully to the north, having lost nine men swept overboard. It was a foretaste for Magellan of the far worse conditions he was to meet in years to come off the coast of Patagonia: an education in the hazards of voyaging in the Southern Hemisphere where wind and wave have a sustained ferocity undreamed of in the kindlier seaways of the north.

After tacking up the Mozambique Channel the fleet dropped anchor off the Primieras Islands, where they reprovisioned and careened. They were ready now to put into effect Dom Manuel's grand strategy: to drive the Arab traders from the Indian Ocean, to blockade the Red Sea and the Persian Gulf, and to set up a chain of fortified posts along the coast of Africa; this, it was hoped, would channel all trade between Europe and the East into Portuguese vessels sailing out of Portuguese ports. And if, over the next few years, Magellan's career in the Indian Ocean seems somewhat confused and difficult to follow, we should remember that the various blockades, sackings and battles he took part in were all directed to putting this grand strategy into effect.

It was over the stern of a ship such as this that enormous waves, shrouded in mist and snow threatened to engulf Almeida's fleet as it neared the Cape of Good Hope.

For the sake of simplicity his years in the East can be divided into four periods: his time in East Africa, his time in India, his time in and around Malacca, and his voyage to the 'Ocean no Christian man as yet had entered into'.

He spent eighteen months in East Africa, and it was here that he first made a name for himself as a man of action, 'a sword quick to chastise the Infidel'. A biographer describes the sort of chastisement he handed out:

After the capture of Kilwa, the Portuguese swooped swiftly on the subsidiary ports; their caravels appeared in the harbours, their boats rowed ashore and the men indulged in an all-out orgy of plunder and rape. The Arabs were slaughtered, their harems were overrun, and by the time the caravels were recalled the entire coast had been devastated, its towns were in ashes and the only Arab survivors were the few who had fled to the jungle.

History does not relate what Magellan thought of these massacres. We know, from the way he acted when he had a command of his own, that he was averse to unnecessary bloodshed; and he was, according to the conscience of his times, a devout Christian. On the other hand the Portuguese had a long-standing blood-feud with Islam, and the probability is that he regarded ravaging Muslim cities and Muslim women as all part of a good day's work.

Having destroyed the Arab centres of commerce and set up their own, the Portuguese proceeded to blockade the coast, with the objective of forcing trade into channels they could control. The man in charge of this blockading was Nuno Pereira, an able young commander who seems to have been the first to spot Magellan's potential; for in December 1505 he promoted him to 'pilot's assistant' aboard his *bergantym*. This *bergantym* was a shallow-draught oar-propelled barge, rowed by Kaffir slaves and armed with six carronades. It proved the scourge of the blockade runners, who, in defiance of the Portuguese, continued to run their goods secretly ashore, for it was fast enough to catch them and powerful enough to blow them clean out of the water with a single broadside. At the end of fifteen months of coastal patrolling Magellan had sunk more than two hundred dhows, and there was now little he did not know about inshore seamanship and warfare.

In the summer of 1507 Pereira was transferred to the Malabar Coast and appointed second-in-command of the Portuguese

Eastern fleet. Magellan went with him. The rival forces of the Crescent and the Cross were now massing for the series of naval encounters which were to determine who should control the trade routes of the East. The protagonists in these far-off but far from unimportant battles were a handful of Portuguese caravels – there were seldom more than twenty-five to thirty in the whole of the Indian Ocean – and a polyglot armada of more than a thousand Arab dhows and Indian *zambucos*. The caravels were good sailers but poor rowers; they were stoutly built, and had, for their day, a devastating fire-power. The dhows and *zambucos*, in contrast, were good rowers but poor sailers; they were lightly built, their timbers being held in place by wooden pegs and coconut-fibre lashings; and they had few guns, for the very good reason that when they fired, their lashings shook loose and the ships quite literally fell apart at the seams. Portuguese tactics were therefore to fight by gunfire at long range, while their opponents attempted to close in, grapple and board.

These engagements built up to a climax in the early weeks of 1509. Almeida's son had been killed in a skirmish off Dabul, and the Viceroy, bent on revenge, got together every available ship and man. Appearing unexpectedly off Dabul, he not only put the garrison to the sword but massacred every living person – man, woman and child – who was in the city. The walls were blown up, the houses levelled and the rubble razed by fire. So savage indeed was the rape of this once prosperous trading centre that it is remembered today by the Muslim curse, 'May the wrath of the Portuguese fall on you as it did upon Dabul.'

Almeida then sought out the Arab fleet. He found it not far from the island of Diu, a straggling armada of more than two hundred ships and twenty thousand men. The Viceroy had only nineteen ships and 1,800 men, but he attacked at once. In the early stages of the encounter Almeida was able to keep to windward and to inflict heavy damage on the dhows and *zambucos* by gunfire; in the afternoon, however, the wind dropped, the two fleets drifted together, and in the series of hand-to-hand engagements which followed, the Portuguese were hard pressed to survive. Realising that a desperate situation called for a desperate remedy, Pereira ordered his caravel to close with the Arab flagship, a massive dhow defended by eight hundred Mamelukes in chain-mail – the personal bodyguard of the Sultan of Egypt. The two vessels grappled like wildcats in what was probably the bloodiest ship-to-ship encounter in naval

'The two vessels grappled like wildcats in what was probably the bloodiest ship-to-ship encounter in naval history'

28

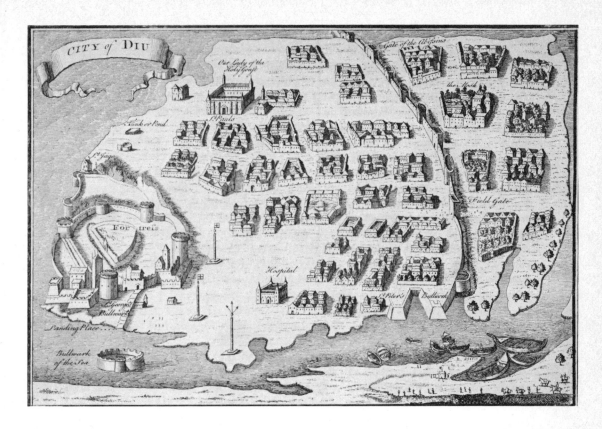

City of Diu

history. At the end of two hours' fighting the crew of the dhow, including the eight hundred Mamelukes, had been killed literally to the last man; the flagship was captured; and as the Cross replaced the Crescent at her masthead, the armada of Islam, disheartened, broke off an encounter which had already cost them a hundred ships and upwards of nine thousand men. Portuguese losses were, in proportion, almost as heavy. The bodies of the Knights of Christ were stacked ten feet high round the mast of the Arab dhow. Among the dead was Pereira. Among those wounded so seriously that his life was despaired of was Magellan.

Although we do not know the exact nature of his wound – contemporary reports say only that he was injured 'nigh unto death' – it must have been a serious one, since he spent a full five months in the hospital at Cochin. As ill luck would have it, this convalescence came at a time when important changes were taking place in the hierarchy of the East: Almeida was being replaced as Viceroy by Albuquerque. This meant that

During his expedition to India, Almeida encountered the Arab fleet near the island city of Diu. Although the fleet consisted of more than two hundred ships and 20,000 men Almeida attacked with only nineteen ships, and less than two thousand men.

29

when Magellan reported back for duty he found new faces in authority. Almeida was in disgrace, Pereira dead and once again at a critical moment in his life he found himself lacking the patronage which was in the sixteenth century a prerequisite of easy advancement.

He was however a man of some substance now, and after an improbable interlude as a mounted knight chasing elephants in the Malabar hills, he enlisted in a caravel bound for Malacca, on the Malay Peninsula. Malacca, in those days, was on the fringe of the unknown, and from this moment Magellan's exploits are flavoured for the first time with the spice of exploration.

In September 1509 Magellan was aboard the first Portuguese fleet to anchor off Malacca, the port which for half a century had been the Mecca of merchants from the West. One of the caravel captains wrote:

Truly there are more ships in this harbour than in any place on earth. More riches too: for its warehouses are crammed with spice from the Moluccas, rubies from Ceylon, ivory from Thailand, silk and jade from China, and slaves with pointed sticks through their nostrils from the great island [New Guinea] in the east.

In September 1509 Magellan was aboard the first Portuguese fleet to anchor off Malacca on the Malay Peninsula; for half a century this port had been the mecca of merchants from the West. The Sultan of Malacca publicly welcomed the Portuguese with a great display of pomp and affection but in secret, under the prompting of the Arab traders, he plotted to murder them.

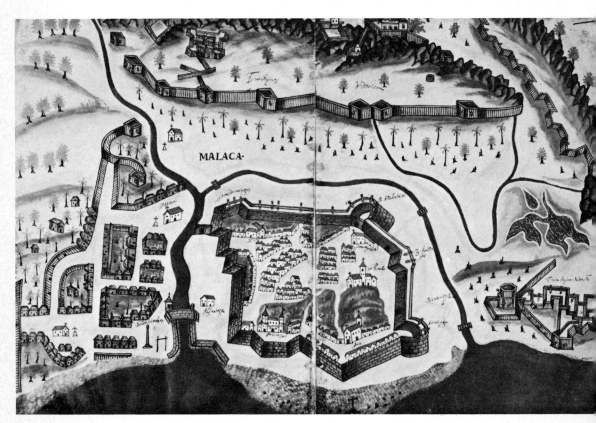

MALACA·

The Sultan of Malacca publicly welcomed the Portuguese with a great display of pomp and affection; but in secret, under the prompting of the Arab traders, he plotted to murder them. Magellan and his cousin Serrano got wind of the plot; but their warnings were taken too lightly and sixty men, including most of the officers, were lured ashore and either captured or killed. The caravels escaped only by the skin of their teeth by cutting through a mass of sampans. One of the last to be hauled aboard was Magellan, who had risked his life to row ashore and pick up his cousin.

A month later he saved Serrano a second time. After being driven from Malacca the Portuguese fleet split up, and Magellan's caravel was on its own when it was overtaken and boarded by a Chinese junk. The Chinese pirates, anticipating an easy victory, came swarming aboard; but the Knights of Christ drove them back and carried the fight on to the deck of their opponent. In the mêlée which followed, the two vessels drifted apart, and Serrano and a handful of men-at-arms suddenly found themselves stranded, hopelessly outnumbered, on the deck of the junk. The captain of the caravel was unable in the heavy seas to bring the two vessels alongside, and it looked as though Serrano and his companions were lost until Magellan and four men-at-arms appeared unexpectedly over the side, took the pirates in the rear and inflicted such slaughter that they surrendered. Magellan had lowered a skiff, and in spite of the seas the five heavily-armed men had managed to row across to the junk and board it unseen.

The pirate ship turned out to be laden with plunder, and Magellan's share amounted to a sizeable fortune. But the captured junk foundered only a few days later in a typhoon. Magellan returned to India, where he took part in an abortive attack on Calicut; here he was wounded a second time, though not seriously. A few months later he was shipwrecked off the Shoals of Papua. While waiting to be rescued, he acted as mediator in an incipient mutiny. And so the sequence of exploring, trading, pillaging and killing continued until, in November 1510, we come to what seems to have been a turning point in Magellan's career: the rape of Goa.

Here is C.M.Parr's description of this tragic event.

In order to enhance the terror of his name among the Moslems, Albuquerque always separated the Arabs from the other inhabitants

Western merchants and travellers flocked to the East to seek their fortune. They sought spice from the Moluccas, rubies from Ceylon, ivory from Thailand, silk and jade from China and slaves from wherever possible. RIGHT a scene of village trading in Java. BELOW AND OPPOSITE Travelling conditions and modes of dress adopted by Europeans in India.

38

of a captured city, and cut off the right hands of the men and the noses and ears of the women. He spared only the comeliest of the girls, whom he reserved as personal gifts for men of influence. At Goa he outdid himself in cruelty, ordering the massacre of every Arab man, woman and child from doddering ancient to newborn babe. This massacre occupied the Portuguese soldiers for three days of systematic search and slaughter, during which they killed over 8,000 people. The Governor-General wrote of these exploits to King Manuel in his official report, giving pious thanks to the Almighty for His aid.

We know Magellan was present at the sack of Goa; we know the plunder wrung from this unfortunate city was enormous – the share set aside for Dom Manuel alone was the equivalent of five million U.S. dollars, while even the lowliest *sobresaliente* was given two years' pay – yet Magellan received not a penny. We are in the realms of conjecture now, for the records are threadbare, but it seems highly probable that Magellan forfeited his share of the booty because he refused to take part in the massacre. Several facts substantiate this theory: Magellan's innate kindness (which will be apparent later from the way he treated his slave), his sense of justice, the fact that none of the records show any trace of payment for his services and, above all, the fact that from this moment he turned his back on warfare and concentrated for the rest of his life on exploration.

His opportunity came shortly after the capture of Malacca in July 1511, an occasion which was marked for Magellan by the acquisition of a slave and a caravel. The former was a Malay boy, about thirteen years old, named Black (or Malacca) Henry, whose loyalty and affection were to be a never-failing source of comfort to Magellan for the rest of his life. The latter was a fine new vessel of more than a hundred tons' burthen, with an experienced crew. Magellan had in fact commanded a caravel before, but this was the first time he was given a free hand to use his ship as he chose. He headed east.

It is at this intriguing moment in his career that we are frustrated by a lack of contemporary records, and the truth is that we do not know for certain where Magellan went. Some chroniclers say that he visited Ternate in the Spice Islands, others that he ventured 'beyond the Spice Islands into seas no Christian man as yet had entered into', and that he discovered a great skein of islands (the Philippines) '600 leagues to the north-east of Malacca'. This latter version seems the more probable, partly because of the letters written to Magellan by his cousin Serrano. Serrano had opted out of the Portuguese feud with Islam and had, a couple of years previously, set himself up in Ternate (in the heart of the Spice Islands) as adviser to the King of Amboina. He was given a large house, a large fortune and a beautiful wife who in due course bore him a large family; here he was to spend the remainder of his life, 'not the most heroic of the conquistadors but surely the wisest and the happiest'. And the point is that Serrano wrote several letters to Magellan begging him to join him in Ternate,

ABOVE When Albuquerque succeeded Almeida as Viceroy of India he began a reign of terror among the Moslems. He always separated the Arabs from the other inhabitants of a captured city and cut off the right hands of the men and the noses and the ears of the women.

OPPOSITE ABOVE A plan of Goa about the middle of the sixteenth century. This was a large and well-defended city, a territorial power of some importance and a strong naval base. Many Europeans came to Goa as it was the principal eastern terminus for the sea-borne trade in spices.

OPPOSITE BELOW The market place of Goa. On this tiny island Albuquerque outdid himself in cruelty, ordering the massacre of every Arab man, woman and child. The massacre occupied the Portuguese soldiers for three days of systematic search and slaughter, during which they killed over 8,000 people.

and the wording of these letters is *not* the wording he would have used had he been describing his environs to someone who already knew them – 'I have found a New World,' he wrote, 'richer, greater and more beautiful than that of Vasco da Gama. . . . I beg you to join me here, that you may sample for yourself the delights which surround me.' The inference is obvious: that Magellan was a stranger to the delights of Serrano's paradise.

Whatever his landfall, the report he handed in on his return created a furore and led to his being relieved of his command and packed off to Lisbon in disgrace. For he put forward the suggestion that the lands he had discovered lay to the east of the Tordesillas[1] line of demarcation, and therefore belonged not to Dom Manuel of Portugal but to King Charles of Spain. It is hardly surprising after this that the Portuguese authorities regarded Magellan as a troublemaker whose theories, if proved right, could jeopardise the whole Portuguese empire in the East.

Magellan must have known that his report would cause a furore, and the fact that he not only put forward such a contentious theory but stuck to it rigidly in the face of official disapproval indicates another facet of his character. He was obstinate as a mule: the sort of man who would deem it a matter of honour never to trim his sails to the wind.

Indeed by the end of his eight years' apprenticeship in the East Magellan had already displayed most of the virtues and vices which were in the years to come to make him so stormy a petrel. This moment in his career is therefore, perhaps, an appropriate one to summarise what sort of man he was.

In appearance – assuming always that we can believe his sixteenth-century portraitists – he was short, thickset and weather-beaten: rugged rather than handsome. According to all the evidence he was as tough as he looked. He was a magnificent practical seaman, and he possessed in abundance that quality beloved by naval officers' selection boards – leadership. As evidence of this, in less than eight years he had risen from *sobresaliente* to captain, and what is more had risen by ability rather than patronage. As regards more personal qualities, the one which springs immediately to mind is courage. He was physically brave to the point of recklessness, and mentally brave to the point of pigheadedness – having once expressed an opinion or embarked on a course nothing would persuade him to deviate

'Magellan must have known that his report would cause a furore'

[1] In 1494 the Treaty of Tordesillas divided the world between Portugal and Spain, giving the former (very roughly) Africa, India, Indonesia and the tip of Brazil, and the latter the rest of America and the Pacific.

A drawing of the young Magellan, who during an eight-year apprenticeship in the East had risen from a midshipman to captain. Lacking patronage he had achieved promotion through personal ability – which was a far removal from the order of the day.

or compromise. He was, in short, a man of decision – though the decisions he arrived at were not always the right ones – a man of incipient greatness.

At this particular moment in time (the spring of 1513) his talents were largely latent, for he was a leader without a cause. But already at the back of his mind was the germ of the idea through which he was to achieve immortality. He was determined to go back to the Philippines. The question was how?

2 The Outsider

IN THE YEARS Magellan had been in the East, the port of Lisbon had emerged even more emphatically as Europe's emporium. Arriving that April morning on the same tide as his caravel were more than a dozen vessels from all over the known world – a squadron of galleys from Southampton, three ships from Palermo and Genoa, a pair of trading *naos* from North Africa and a slaving caravel from the Ivory Coast. The water-front which a decade earlier had consisted of meadowland and fishing villages was lined with docks, warehouses and yards; while symbolic of the links which now bound Portugal to the sea was the royal palace, with its plaza and stairways sweeping directly up from the water.

One might have thought that so thriving a metropolis would welcome home adventurers who, like Magellan, were the instruments of her prosperity. But the truth is that Lisbon in 1513 was no place for a simple man of action. It was a place where men played politics, manipulated trade and made money out of the endeavours of those in far-off continents; no place, in other words, for Magellan. He was put on half-pay, with the nominal rank of *fidalgo escudeira*, and refused a place in the next expedition to the East. To add to his troubles, the moneylender to whom he had entrusted a considerable part of the fortune he had won in the East absconded, and he now found himself not only out of work but out of pocket. It was a combination of these circumstances which led him, in the late summer of 1513, to volunteer for service in Morocco where the Portuguese were intent on destroying the power of their traditional enemies the Moors.

Magellan's year in North Africa was nothing if not eventful. He was given a good post: that of *Quadrilheiro Mor*, the man responsible for the safeguarding and ransoming of prisoners of war and booty. This position he owed to the patronage of Count John de Meneses and John of Lisbon, both of whom seem to have been favourably impressed by Magellan's ability and energy. Indeed his relationship with the navigator John of Lisbon quickly developed into a personal friendship which was to lead indirectly to the great climax of his life, the circumnavigation of the world.

John of Lisbon was the foremost navigator in Portugal, in ability if not in rank. He seems to have been much the same sort of man as Magellan: a first-class practical seaman, but lacking in social grace and tact – he was once heard to refer to his staff of noblemen's sons as 'a pack of perfumed poltroons'. In the

PREVIOUS PAGES Ships in the bustling harbour of Lisbon which was the home port for much of the shipping which brought back riches from the East.

summer of 1513 he had been given the job of transporting the Portuguese army from Lisbon to Azamur on the north coast of Africa, a task which he performed with dispatch and efficiency, without the loss of a man. Magellan was his aide, and during the brief voyage to Azamur the two shared a cabin in the Portuguese flagship.

They seem to have got on well from the start. John of Lisbon's voyages and discoveries had been mostly in the West, Magellan's mostly in the East. It would have been fascinating to eavesdrop as the two greatest mariners of their age exchanged reminiscences. In view of what happened later, it would seem reasonable to suppose that, it was now (in the third week in August 1513) that Magellan first conceived the idea of returning to his beloved Philippines not east through the Indian Ocean but west through the little-known reaches of the Atlantic.

This, however, was in the future. The immediate consequences of the Moroccan campaign were not so fortunate for Magellan. He was wounded a third time – and seriously – and very nearly court-martialled.

The fact that he saw action at all in North Africa calls for comment. Magellan was now thirty-five – past his prime for those days; his position as *Quadrilheiro Mor* was an executive one, and it might have been supposed that he would see little actual fighting. On the contrary, we know that his horse was killed under him during the assault on Azamur, and that defending the city some six months later he received a lance wound in the right knee which made him lame for life. The inference is that he rather enjoyed a scrap, a predilection which was eventually to cost him his life.

His court-martial was an affair of some complexity. The Moroccan campaign of 1513-14 was successful, and there were prisoners and booty in abundance. It was Magellan's task to dispose of these and to distribute the proceeds, and since no records were kept the path to corruption was wide open. Inevitably, in his parcelling out of the spoils, Magellan made enemies, and as ill luck would have it one of these was the influential Pedro de Sousa. In the spring of 1514 de Sousa preferred charges against Magellan, alleging, according to some accounts, that he 'sold for personal profit 30 sheep', and according to others that he 'entered into collusion with the Moors and resold them 400 horses'. It is difficult at this distance in time to arrive at the truth; but neither of the charges when examined in detail strikes

'Magellan conceived the idea of returning to his beloved Philippines west through the little-known reaches of the Atlantic'

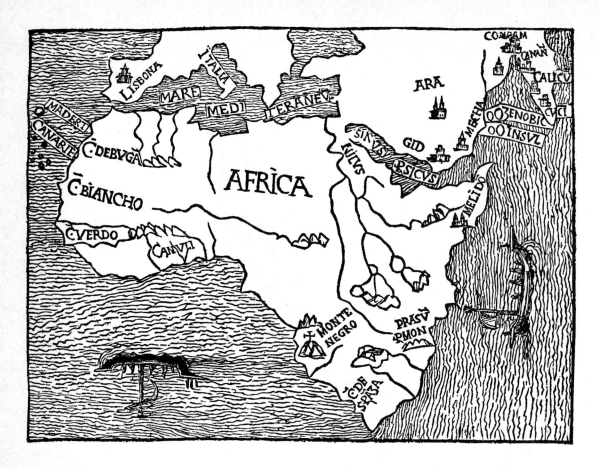

A woodcut map of Africa from Montalboddo's *Itinerarius Portugallesium e Lusitania in India* printed in Milan in 1508, and showing the Portuguese sea route to India.

one as convincing. As regards the first, if Magellan had wanted to steal something he would surely have selected a more valuable objective than a couple of dozen sheep; and as regards the second, he would have been crazy to indulge in treason when so many less dangerous deals could have been concluded without the connivance of the Moors. There is also the point that when eventually the case was brought to court neither charge could be made to stick. It was an episode, however, which disillusioned Magellan still further, and he made up his mind to take the first opportunity of returning to the East.

The year which followed – 1516 – was probably the most miserable in Magellan's life. All summer he hung about the palace, still on half-pay, trying vainly to secure command of a caravel bound for the Orient. But he found the shoals of Court politics more devious (and indeed more dangerous) than the shoals of the Far Eastern seas. He was no sycophant; the arts of flattery and ingratiation were alien to his character which, for all its flaws, was essentially open and honest; and in the autumn, realising that he was getting nowhere by indirect methods, he decided to risk everything on a direct approach to the King. Here is Stefan Zweig's account of the débâcle taken from his biography, *Conqueror of the Seas* which followed:

Magellan therefore sought audience of the king, thus choosing the most unlucky path a man can choose at court – the honest and direct one. King Manuel received him in the same throne-room, perhaps sitting on the same throne as that in which his predecessor John II had refused Columbus's proposal. In the identical spot was acted out an identical scene.... We can picture the lame fidalgo limping awkwardly up to the king and handing him papers to prove that, in North Africa, he had been accused falsely. We can picture him putting his first request: that in view of his long service [which he unwisely recited] and his third wound, his pension might now be increased by half-a-crusado [in modern coinage a little less than 5p] a month. This was a ludicrously small demand; and it was almost inconceivable that so proud and ambitious a man as Magellan should have had to bend the knee for such a trifle. The king, nevertheless, frowned as he stared at the petitioner. It probably annoyed him that instead of humbly begging a favour, Magellan seemed to be demanding a right. He signified his refusal.

If Magellan had been wise he would now have withdrawn, since the king's angry countenance did not augur well for further favours. But instead of quitting the throne-room, Magellan stood his ground and began to put his second request, which was the one he had most at heart. He asked whether the monarch could not offer him some worthy post in the royal service, since he felt too young and vigorous to spend the rest of his life as a court petitioner and recipient of alms. Ships sailed to Africa and to the Indies on almost every tide, and nothing would seem more reasonable than that the command of one of these ships should be given to the man who knew the eastern sea routes as well as anyone alive. King Manuel, however, coldly refused, indicating that there was no position whatsoever for Magellan in the service of the Portuguese crown. When the mariner asked leave to seek employment elsewhere, the reply was brutal in its finality.

'Serve whom you will, Clubfoot. It is a matter of indifference to us.'

If these rebuffs were hard to bear, the humiliation to come, when Dom Manuel refused the kiss of fealty, must have been unendurable. Zweig makes no exaggerated claim when he says that Magellan, at the end of this nightmare audience, left the palace 'a broken and rejected beggar'.

'He was no sycophant; the arts of flattery and ingratiation were alien to his character'

43

The Spanish Coat of Arms. Magellan had become pre-occupied with the idea of sailing to the Philippines not east via the Indian Ocean but west across the Atlantic so, after losing favour with Portugal's Dom Manuel he turned to the lions and castles of Castile for patronage.

That night, aboard the merchantman bound for Minho, he must have taken stock of his situation and been close to despair. For twenty years he had served his country with loyalty and distinction: as clerk, *sobresaliente*, soldier, navigator, sea captain and administrator. He had proved himself, by land and by sea, under desert stars and tropic sun, a bold, resourceful and, what is more, a successful commander. But no one now would give him a command: no one, that is, in Portugal.

It was probably during the course of this night, when his fortunes were at their nadir and the stars in their courses seemed to offer him not the slightest glimmer of comfort, that Magellan first thought of transferring his allegiance to Spain.

44

There were two ideas now at the back of his mind: that of sailing to the Philippines not east by the Indian Ocean but west by the Atlantic, and that of sailing not under the *guinas* of Portugal but under the lions and castles of Castile. All that was needed was a catalyst to transform these two ideas into a single reality.

Arriving at Porto in the north of Portugal, Magellan went to 'a small mariners' tavern close to the waterfront'. Porto, in 1516, was crowded with out-of-work seamen, many of whom, like Magellan, were veterans of the East. Because of their poverty, their unfashionable clothes and their conversation of things and places beyond the ken of the stay-at-homes, these

Magellan longed for a ship of his own. His frustration grew as vessels such as this sixteenth-century carrack left Lisbon on almost every tide. Yet because of Dom Manuel's dislike of him he was denied a command.

45

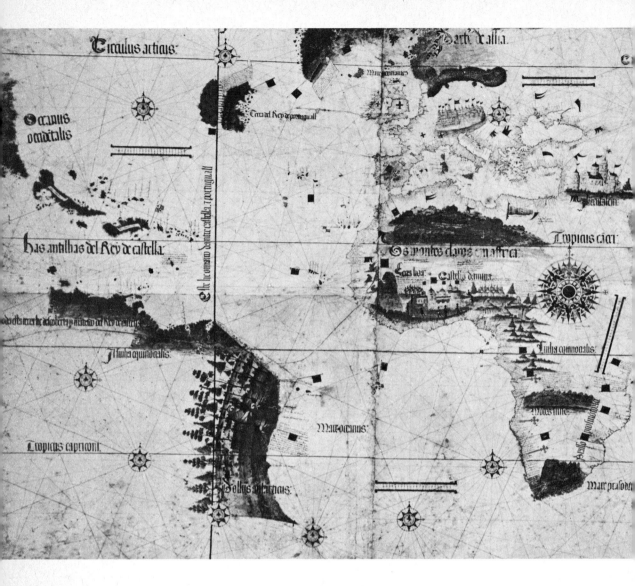

Circulus articus· · Oart' rasia·
Oceanus occidtalis
has antilhas del Rey de castella·
flinha equinotialis·
Tropicus capricom·
Sellus meridialis·
Os montes daros en affrica·
Tropicus cicr·
linha equinotialis·
Marocanus·
Mare persodm·

men tended to be ostracised by genteel society, and Parr gives us a graphic vignette of how Magellan must have felt in these the darkest hours of his life:

    Night after night he sat in the noisy torch-lit taproom of the tavern, feeling a man apart. In imagination he was far from Porto, steering his caravel once more through Malayan archipelagos teeming with camphor, sandalwood and mace. Perhaps he thought of the storms of the Indian Ocean or the rushing currents of the Indonesian straits. Then, abruptly, he would come back to the present, drain his tankard,

This Cantin world map, published in 1502, was one of the many versions of the then-known world. It shows the line of demarcation agreed

upon by the Kings of Spain
and Portugal in the Treaty of
Tordesillas in 1494. The flags
of both countries are shown
flying over their territory.

and limp off into the darkness, knowing himself to be a master-mariner without a ship, a cavalier without a mount.

In this winter of his discontent Magellan had only two sources of comfort: the devotion of his slave and, in the early weeks of 1517, the two hundred crusados which his lawyer at last managed to extract from the defaulting moneylender. It was at this turning-point in his life that he came under the influence of three men, all of whom exerted pressure on him to transfer his allegiance to Spain: Ruy de Faleira, John of Lisbon and Duarte Barbosa, the King's scrivener.

Ruy de Faleira was the leading Portuguese astronomer of his day. He was a contemporary of Magellan's; they had, as boys, been pages together in Queen Leonora's Court. Now, twenty-five years later, they found themselves with another bond in common – they had both been ostracised by Dom Manuel. For in 1516 Faleira had applied for the position of astronomer royal, but had been passed over in favour of a less erudite but more courtly applicant. He came north to join the colony of discontented seamen at Porto, while his brother Francisco crossed the border into Spain and was at once offered a first-class position as 'hydrographer and nautical adviser' to the *Casa de Antillas* (a maritime hierarchy controlling trade with the East). After a couple of months Francisco wrote to his brother suggesting that he join him. Faleira, by this time, had struck up a friendship with Magellan. They were an unlikely pair: the reserved, taciturn man of action, and the loquacious, highly-strung intellectual. But they had two things in common: they could neither of them find employment in Portugal to match their talents, and they were both passionately devoted to the advancement of geography – Magellan as a practical explorer and Faleira as a theoretical astronomer and navigator. It was perhaps because their talents were in the same field and yet so divergent that they got on, initially, very well. They had a lot to teach one another; and without doubt the idea of crossing into Spain was given an airing during their discussions.

Initially this idea probably appealed to Faleira more than to Magellan, but in the spring of 1517 the latter had a visitor who was to change the course of his life. For early that March there put into the mouth of the Douro a seaman who was no out-of-work, out-of-favour malcontent, but the most renowned navigator of his age: John of Lisbon. And he had come specifically to see Magellan.

It seems probable that there was a good deal of sympathy for
Magellan among the seafaring fraternity at Lisbon; they felt he
had been hardly done by – as indeed he had. John of Lisbon in
particular was genuinely distressed at the treatment meted out
to a colleague he held in high regard, and as soon as he had paid
off from his voyage he sailed secretly to Porto to bring his friend
up to date on recent developments in the Atlantic. More landfalls had been made in the Caribbean, the coast of America had
been mapped from the equator to the twentieth parallel and
John of Lisbon himself had followed the coast of Brazil southward until he discovered a great headland (Cape Santa Maria)
at the same latitude as the Cape of Good Hope. Rounding this
he had come to a reach of water running west-south-west as far
as the eye could see. This, he decided, must surely be the much
sought *el paso*, the strait which led by way of the Great South
Sea to the Islands of Spice.

To appreciate the significance of this presumed discovery we
need to know a little of how the men of the early sixteenth century visualised the world they lived in.

All educated and well-informed men knew, in Magellan's
day, that the world was a sphere – they had known this, at least
in theory, for the last 1,500 years – but they believed its circum-
ference to be very much less than in fact it is. Columbus, for
example, mistook the West Indies for the East Indies: that is to
say the world as *he* pictured it, was a world minus the Americas
and the Pacific (i.e. a world only half its actual size). In the early
years of the sixteenth century, as more and more landfalls were
made in the far reaches of the Atlantic and it became clear that
these landfalls were not part of the hoped-for Spice Islands, it
gradually dawned on both seamen and cartographers that an
unexpected land mass blocked their way. This land mass, however, was not visualised as a continuous coastline running without a break very nearly from pole to pole – no such coastline
existed in the Old World, so why should it have been envisaged
in the New? During the first two decades of the century seamen
were therefore expecting any moment to find a way through this
troublesome land mass; once they had located such a way
through, they imagined their troubles would be over and that
the Islands of Spice would be 'no more than a couple of days'
sailing to the West'. For they had no cognizance of the vastness
of the Pacific.

We can imagine, therefore, how excited Magellan must have

LA MER DV SV:

TROPIQVE

MER PACIFIQVE
OV DE MAGELLAN

been when John of Lisbon told him, in the spring of 1517, that he had actually found such a way through this land mass: *el paso*, a broad deepwater strait which he had followed for more than a hundred miles and which ran west-south-west as far as the eye could see. He had not, it is true, sailed all the way through this passage and into the ocean beyond, but he had taken note of its latitude and longitude and its currents, tides, soundings, shoals, anchorage and landmarks. He had also brought back from its shores a valuable cargo of dyes, silver ornaments and slaves, and for good measure he passed on to Magellan the information that the Indians who lived by the northern shore of this strait had told him of 'a great mountain

These maps were drawn for Henry II of France in the first half of the sixteenth century. The world in those days was believed to be far smaller than it actually is and far more precisely balanced. It was thought that everything had to be symmetrical; that the northern land mass had to be balanced in the south and that continents like Africa and America had to terminate at nearly the same latitude.

50

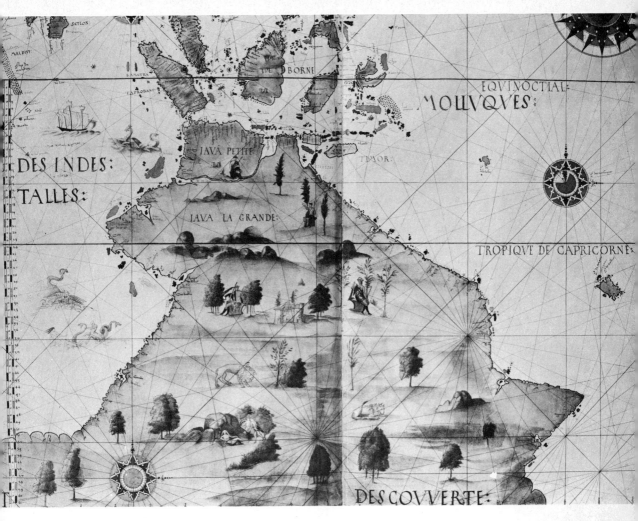

of solid silver'[1] from which they could obtain inexhaustible
supplies.

Magellan must have questioned John of Lisbon closely about
these discoveries; and he must in particular have raised the
point that since the west-reaching seaway had not been followed
all the way through, no one could be certain that it was indeed
el paso. We can only guess at John of Lisbon's answer; but in
view of what happened later it was probably something like
this: 'Even if this particular seaway is not *el paso*, you need only
follow the coast a few miles farther and you will come to the
most southerly point of the land mass; you will then be able to
sail round the bottom of the continent in the same way that

[1] What the Indians failed to get across to John of Lisbon was that this
mountain, the Potosi complex in Bolivia, lay not adjacent to the coast, but
more than a thousand miles through near-impenetrable jungle to the
north-west.

TOP LEFT Henry the
Navigator, third son of King
John I of Portugal, devoted
his life to furthering explora-
tions by sea. The school
of navigation and map-
making which he established
at Sagres brought together
the greatest experts of the
time, and their work laid the
foundations for the success
of the early Portuguese
voyages.

TOP RIGHT Vasco da Gama
who in 1498 discovered the
sea route from Europe
to India.

BELOW LEFT King John II of
Portugal, called the Perfect,
who continued the work of
his great-uncle, Henry the
Navigator.

Dias, a generation earlier, sailed round the bottom of Africa.'

To understand the logic behind such an argument, we need to take a further look at the way men in those days thought of the world. They thought of it not only as a small sphere, but as a precisely balanced one: that is to say not only did they fail to appreciate its size, they failed also to appreciate the haphazard nature of its layout of land and sea. They thought that everything had to be symmetrical: that the northern land mass had to be balanced in the south (hence the *Terra Australis Incognita* which was to feature on every globe for the next 250 years) and that continents like Africa and America had to terminate at very nearly the same latitude. If a mapmaker had suggested in 1517 that virtually the whole of the southern hemisphere would turn out to be sea, and that the coast of America would extend more than a thousand miles farther south than the coast of Africa, he would have been laughed to scorn. So when John of Lisbon sailed down the coast of America and discovered a great south-facing headland at 35° south – the exact latitude of the Cape of Good Hope – and when he rounded this headland and found open water running for more than a hundred miles westward, he naturally assumed that he had done one of two things: either he had discovered *el paso*, or he had discovered the southernmost tip of the new-found continent.

The news of this momentous if, as we now know, fallacious discovery rekindled the idea which had been lying fallow for some time at the back of Magellan's mind: the idea of returning to the Philippines by sailing not east but west.

There was nothing especially original about this idea – it was in essence the idea which had led Columbus in 1492 to the Caribbean. What *was* original about the voyage which Magellan now began seriously to contemplate was that he knew very well that the land mass of America blocked his path, but that he believed he had secret information which would enable him to find a way through (or round) this land.

This belief seemed to be confirmed during his visit to the royal *Tesoraria* (map-room) which John of Lisbon arranged for him in late April or early May. For it was during this visit that he first studied the Martin Behaim globe.

Martin Behaim, or Martin of Bohemia as some reports describe him, was Court cartographer to Dom Manuel. He was in charge of the map-room to which, by royal decree, every mariner returning from the Atlantic was obliged to bring his

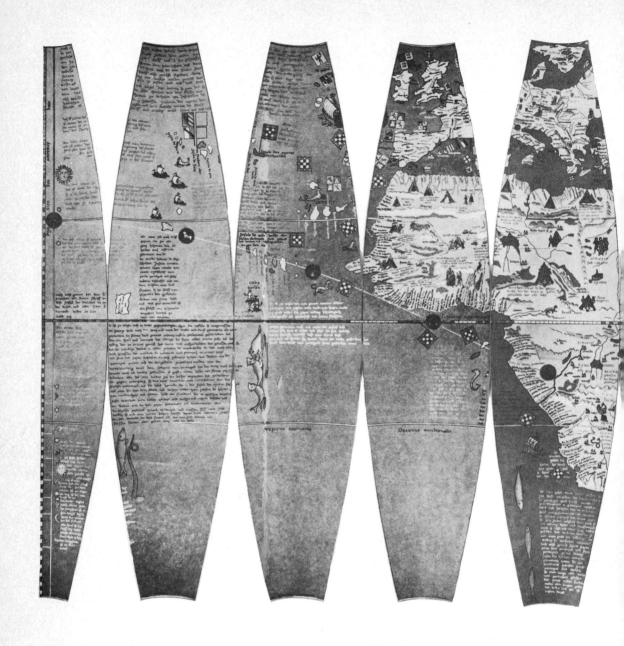

The German navigator and geographer Martin Behaim constructed this
terrestrial globe in 1492. He was Court cartographer to John II of
Portugal, and it was probably in the royal map-room in Lisbon that
Magellan studied his globe.

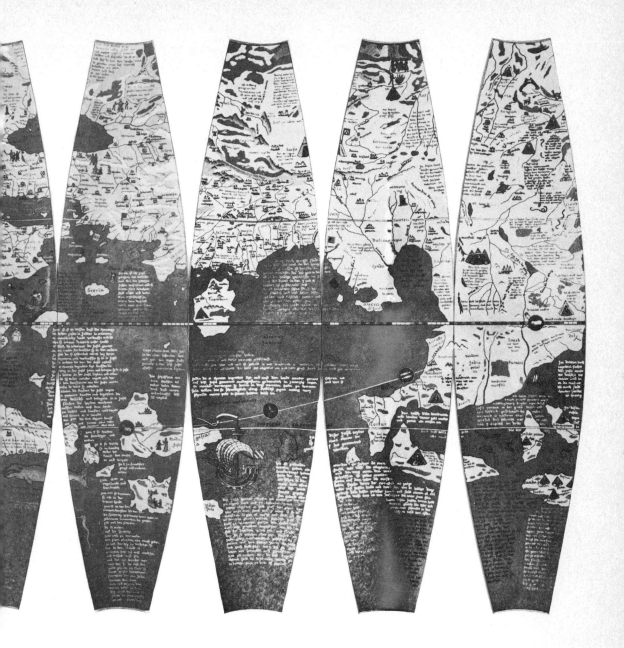

charts, globes, logbooks, diaries and secret reports. No man had had a greater knowledge of the western ocean; and not only had he stored and collated the reports of the returning seamen, he used them to compile maps of his own. The most famous of these was the Martin Behaim globe of 1506, completed only a few months before his death. This globe was different from any previously constructed in that it showed a strait in the exact position of John of Lisbon's supposed *el paso*. Magellan must have been impressed, for he either purloined the original or had it copied and smuggled out the replica.

What Dom Manuel would have done had he known that his foremost navigator had given the ostracised Magellan this top-secret information can only be guessed at. Nor does the fact that the information turned out eventually to be fallacious diminish the risk that Magellan's friends took. He must have returned to Porto that summer in a happier frame of mind than he had been in for years. For the voyage on which he had set his heart now began to look eminently feasible. All that he needed was a patron.

'The voyage began to look eminently feasible. All he needed was a patron'

It was at this critical moment in his life that he had a long overdue stroke of good fortune. He was visited, quite unexpectedly, by the man who was to introduce him to both his wife and his patron: his erstwhile friend from India, the King's scrivener Duarte Barbosa.

Barbosa arrived in Porto in either June or July. He had returned to Lisbon from the East earlier in the year, and had met the same frigid reception as Magellan. Deciding there was no future for him in Portugal, he went to visit his uncle Diogo Barbosa who had married into the Andalusian nobility and was living in style in Seville. Diogo Barbosa was a man of some standing in Spain, and not only on account of his marriage, for he was in charge of the Royal Arsenals on the Guadalquivir. He urged his nephew to join him permanently. The Barbosas were a gifted and attractive pair: wealthy, shrewd, knowledgeable and dedicated to exploration in general and the development of the Spice Islands in particular. They seem to have known about John of Lisbon's discoveries in South America, and to have hit on the idea of fitting out a private expedition of their own to pioneer a new route to the Isles of Spice by way of John of Lisbon's strait. They decided to offer the command of their expedition to Magellan, and it was to put this proposition to him that Barbosa landed secretly at the mouth of the Douro.

Magellan did not hesitate. He agreed to join Barbosa in Spain.

Here, not only was he accorded a welcome by the authorities far warmer than he had ever received in his own country, within a few weeks of his arrival he found himself betrothed to Diogo Barbosa's daughter, 'the fair Beatriz whose comeliness was matched only by the size of her dowry!' Fortune, to whom he had for so long been a stranger, was smiling on him at last.

3 The Spanish Venture

Ｍ AGELLAN LEFT PORTO on 12 October 1517. He was never to set foot in Portugal again.

A week later he stepped ashore at Seville, where he was met by Diogo Barbosa, who took him at once to his palatial residence on the banks of the Guadalquivir. Here he met Beatriz, to whom, by arrangement, he was to be married.

The marriage turned out to be none the less happy for being an affair of the head and not, initially, of the heart. No details of the wedding ceremony have survived, and no description of Beatriz; all we know is that she was in her twenties, comely, accomplished and quite staggeringly rich. The indications are that she and Magellan became genuinely fond of each other. In the two years they were together she bore him two children, and although it would be wrong to overemphasise the part she played in shaping his career, her love did provide a brief, almost idyllic *divertissement* amid the stormy passages of his life.

Magellan's first couple of months in Spain were spent at Seville, with his father-in-law introducing him to influential members of society and pulling all possible strings to obtain royal approval and financial backing for their expedition. By the end of the year three important people had become involved in their plans: Juan de Aranda, chief factor to the *Casa de Antillas*, Bishop Fonseca, President of the Council of the Indies, and Cristobal de Haro, a German banker who probably knew more about the Spice Islands in general and the pepper trade in particular than anyone alive. The involvement of these men of standing led, inevitably, to the expedition becoming a political football, kicked around to advance the prestige of its benefactors; and this in turn led to intrigue, duplicity, ill-feeling and all the ills that stem from a divided structure of command.

It would have been a great deal better had Barbosa been able to finance the expedition privately and dispatch it secretly. This, however, proved impossible because of the enormous expense involved and the fact that all expeditions had to receive royal approval, never granted easily. Magellan was fortunate to be offered an almost immediate audience with the King, which was to take place at Valladolid on the plateau of the *Tierra de Campos*.

It was a historic confrontation: the pale, slightly-built youth of seventeen, the weather-beaten veteran of forty, and round them the Cardinals, councillors and interpreters of the Spanish Court. At first King Charles was suspicious; he had had dealings

PREVIOUS PAGES With the promise of a ship for his voage to the Philippines, Magellan forsook his native Portugal and took up Spanish allegiance. In October 1517 he entered Seville, by the River Guadalquivir, sailing past the 'Golden Tower' – still standing when this scene was engraved in the early nineteenth century.

OPPOSITE A typical Arab camel caravan. The Arabs, who were in a strong geographical position, had dominated the trade from the East for centuries. It was partly to gain control of this lucrative trade, and partly to outflank Islam, that Portugal and Spain searched for a new way to the East.

with Portuguese renegades before, men anxious to legitimise their maraudings into Portugal's far-flung possessions, and he questioned Magellan closely about the exact location of the islands he was hoping to reach. Magellan answered the King's questions frankly and with authority; he showed him the Behaim globe, 'borrowed' for just such an occasion from the map-room in Lisbon; and on the strength of this globe and his favourable impression of Magellan, Charles commissioned the voyage on the spot.

Magellan's petition had been sedulously rehearsed and adroitly presented, but even in his wildest dreams he could hardly have hoped for such immediate and unqualified success. It was not perhaps surprising that the King was initially won over: with the body of a middle-aged invalid and the mind of a young man of action, Charles was peculiarly susceptible to ad-

Magellan's destination – the Philippines and the Spice Islands, which he hoped to reach by a new and shorter route.

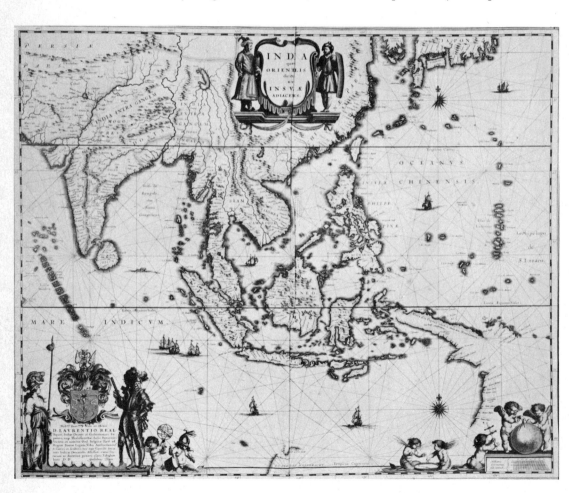

venturous projects. What *was* surprising was that the King not only drew up and signed on the spot a charter which was almost ridiculously favourable to Magellan, but that he stood by him staunchly throughout the vicissitudes of eighteen months' commissioning.

Charles I has often been accused by historians of indecision, vacillation and 'a chronic inability to pursue a constant and straightforward course'. Yet his treatment of Magellan was perfectly straightforward. In the face of bitter and sustained political pressure, the young King never failed to give the mariner less than his wholehearted and unqualified support. Why? It has been suggested that there was a bond between the two men: that they liked, respected and trusted one another. (Waterfront gossip disseminated by the Portuguese alleged that Magellan seduced the boy-King, but this need be taken no

The cabal who financed Magellan's voyage: Aranda, Fonseca and Cristobal de Haro. Their objective was to discover a quick, new and hence more profitable route to the Spice Islands.

more seriously than the story that he, Magellan, had been sired by the devil and hence had a cloven hoof.) It has also been suggested that Charles was favourably impressed by Magellan's insistence that the islands he was seeking lay in the Spanish rather than the Portuguese sphere of influence. This is true; but it hardly accounts for the remarkable rapport between them.

The truth is that Charles and Magellan saw the expedition through the same eyes. For them its objective was to discover the Philippines and to annex this great and rich new archipelago for Spain. For Aranda, Fonseca and Cristobal de Haro, on the other hand, its objective was to discover a quick, new (and hence more profitable) route to the Spice Islands. In other words the leader and the *deus ex machina* of the expedition were explorers; the cabal who financed it were traders.

This division lay at the root of all the ills by which the fleet was subsequently racked: it brought about misunderstanding, intrigue, treachery, mutiny and violent death. Given the conditions of the time, this may have been almost inevitable. It was none the less tragic.

Initially, however, there was hardly a hint of the vicissitudes to come, and Magellan returned to Seville in high spirits to prepare for the coming voyage – a labour of love, perhaps, but also a labour of Hercules. Here is Stefan Zweig's description of the part which Magellan played in these vital preliminaries:

Whereas the visionary Columbus had left the details of preparing his ships to his pilots, the practical Magellan (who in this matter resembled Napoleon) attended personally to the most mundane minutia. He had an infinite capacity for taking pains. Just as Napoleon, prior to crossing the Alps, carefully calculated how many pounds of powder and sacks of oats should be left at a certain place on a certain day, so did Magellan, when fitting out his fleet, decide for two or three years in advance how best to provide for every conceivable eventuality. This was a tremendous undertaking for one solitary man. No doubt the king had pledged his word to provide all that was needed; but between a royal command and its fulfilment is room for any number of frustrations and delays. . . . Magellan, however, had a deeply-felt sense of responsibility toward the men whose lives would be in his care. He watched every circumstance. He personally inspected the supplies, checked the accounts, examined every rope, timber and weapon aboard his vessels; from masthead to keel he knew them, as well as he knew the palm of his hand. . . . All this was achievement on the heroic scale, demanding almost daimonic powers of involvement and self-sacrifice.

OPPOSITE Map of 1522, the earliest map to name the various islands of the Moluccas. It also shows the Line of Demarcation (the vertical red line) dividing the Spanish and Portuguese spheres of influence. This line was first drawn in the Atlantic, then extended around the globe, but its exact position in the East Indies remained the subject of vigorous dispute.

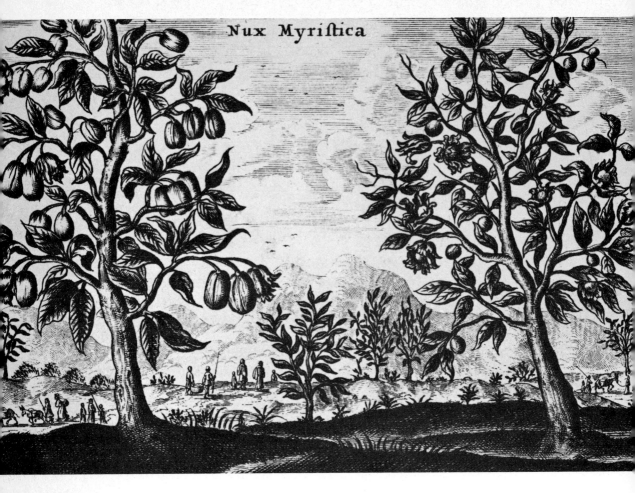

Nux Myriſtica

Even under favourable conditions the commissioning of so important an expedition would have been arduous. And conditions in Seville in 1518 were far from favourable. For Magellan soon discovered that he had enemies. Portuguese agents, in an effort to stop the armada sailing, pilfered supplies and stirred up trouble in the docks. Spanish financiers, anxious to advance the trading aspect of the voyage and retard the exploratory, made continuous efforts to whittle away Magellan's authority. They tried to do this in two ways: by pressuring the King to amend the terms of his charter and by appointing their sympathisers to key positions in the fleet. The latter manœuvre was the more successful; and in next to no time the offices of second-in-command, treasurer and astrologer had been filled by 'friends of the *Casa de Antillas*'. Three out of the five captains

The produce of the Spice Islands included coconuts, palm oil, hemp, cacao, sandalwood, teak, camphor, quinine, dyes, pepper and assorted spices.
ABOVE is a nutmeg tree and OPPOSITE clove trees being harvested.

Caryophyllus   *Naegel Boom*

were also chosen by the Council, as were four out of five pilots, and more than half of the *maestres* (first-lieutenants), *contra-maestres* (boatswains), *alguacils* (masters-at-arms) and *despenseros* (stewards). The type of man appointed was often a time-server, totally unsuited to the position he filled. Typical of this element was his second-in-command, Juan de Cartagena, the natural son of Fonseca (euphemistically known as his 'nephew'), a bombastic and incompetent troublemaker who was plotting mutiny before the fleet was out of sight of land. Almost a third of his ship's companies were, in fact, opposed to the great venture on which they were embarked; and one wonders why so many people went to such lengths in order to hamstring or divert Magellan. The answer lies in the importance of the spice trade.

In the fifteenth century the search for the Spice Islands had

ng it meets withall. The leaues are few in number, ‡ growing at each joint one, firſt on one ſide
the ſtalk, then on the other, like in ſhape to the long vndiuided leaues of Iuy, but thinner, ſharp
ointed, and ſometimes ſo broad that they are foure inches ouer, but moſt commonly two inches
road and foure long, hauing alwaies fiue pretty large nerues running along them. The fruit grow
cluſtering together vpon long ſtalks, which come forth at the joints againſt the leaues, as you may
ſee in the figure: the root (as one may coniecture) is creeping, for the branches that ly on the ground
do at their joints put forth new fibres or roots. Wee are beholden to *Cluſius* for this exact figure
and deſcription, which hee made by certaine branches brought home by the Hollanders from the
Eaſt Indies. The Curious may ſee more hereof in his Exoticks and notes vpon *Garcias*.

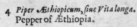

† 3 *Piper longum.*   4 *Piper Æthiopicum, ſiue Vita longa.*
Long Pepper.   Pepper of Æthiopia.

2 The plant that brings white pper is not to be diſtinguiſhed from the other plant, but only
by the colour of the fruit, no more th   Vine that beareth blacke grapes, from that which brings
white: and of ſome it is thought, that the ſelfe ſame plant doth ſomtimes change it ſelf from black
to white, as diuers other plants doe. ‡ Neither *Cluſius*, nor any other elſe that I haue yet met with,
haue deliuered vs any thing of certaine, of the plant whereon white Pepper growes; *Cluſius* onely
hath giuen vs the maner how it growes vpon the ſtalks, as you may ſee it here expreſt. ‡

There is alſo another kind of Pepper, ſeldome brought into theſe parts of Europe, called *Piper
Canarium*: it is hollow within, light, and empty, but good to draw flegme from the head, to help
the tooth-ache and cholericke affects.

3 The tree that beareth long pepper hath no ſimilitude at all with the plant that brings black
and white Pepper: ſome haue deemed them to grow all on one tree; which is not conſonant to
truth: for they grow in countries far diſtant one from another, and alſo that countrey where ther
is blacke Pepper, hath not any of the long Pepper. And therefore *Galen* following *Dioſcorides*, we
together both ouerſeene in this point. This tree, ſaith *Monardus*, is not great, yet
ſtance, diſperſing here and there his claſping tendrels, wherewith it taketh ho
ſuch other things as do grow neere vnto it. The branches are many and twiggy, w
the fruit, conſiſting of many graines growing vpon a ſlender foot-ſtalke, thruſt o

RIGHT A contemporary illustration of pepper harvesting, and ABOVE two
kinds of pepper plant. Pepper was an essential ingredient for meat
preservation in sixteenth-century Europe.

been the dominating factor in exploration, the *leitmotif* of voyages such as Columbus's and Vasco da Gama's. Now that these islands had at last been discovered, the exploitation of them was the dominating factor in trade, the goal not only of seamen and explorers, but also of financiers, politicians, diplomats and kings. Historians have often stressed the importance of this trade; yet few exact definitions of where the Spice Islands were, what their produce consisted of and why it was so important have ever been made. Without this background knowledge, however, it is difficult to appreciate the trade's significance.

A sixteenth-century camel caravan. It consisted of fifty to seventy camels, fastened head to tail by a rope and led by an ass. The gullies and sand dunes of the desert proved ideal terrain for ambush, and the Arabs often found their cargo of pepper snatched from them by marauding robbers.

'The Spiceries' was a phrase coined in the sixteenth century to describe all those islands of present-day Indonesia which produced spice in general and pepper in particular. The geographical centre of these islands was the Moluccas (i.e. Halmahera, Ceram, Amboina, Buru, Obi and Batjam), and around its perimeter lay Tanimbar, Timor, Flores and the Celebes. These islands were all concentrated into a comparatively small area (some six hundred miles square); to European vessels approaching from the west they were screened by the Malay Peninsula and by the bulk of Sumatra, Java and Borneo; they were therefore not only a long way from Europe, they were also extremely difficult to find. Their produce was much the same in the sixteenth century as it is today – coconuts, palm-oil, hemp, cacao, sandalwood, teak, camphor, quinine, dyes, assorted

70

The amusing aspects of the
life of the camel caravan
herder have been well
illustrated in these paintings

The 90-ton *Victoria*: one of
the smaller vessels in
Magellan's fleet and the only
ship to return to Spain.

spices and pepper. The majority of these items were luxuries in
Renaissance Europe, but the last-mentioned was vital.

Pepper does not sound a particularly exciting or essential
commodity today – it lacks the glamour of gold or the usefulness
of wool – yet in sixteenth-century Europe it was for millions of
ordinary people quite literally a necessity of life. The reason for
this lay in the chronic shortage of winter fodder in central and
northern Europe. Because of this shortage over eighty per cent
of all European cattle and sheep had to be slaughtered each
autumn and their carcasses cured. This was done by treating
them with a mixture of salt and pepper, which helped both to
preserve the meat and to disguise its tainted condition. Salt was
readily available. Pepper had to be imported. It would therefore
be no exaggeration to say that the stability of Europe's food
supply depended on this one commodity.

From time immemorial, pepper had been imported into
Europe by spice caravans from the East. This, however, involved a long, dangerous and very expensive journey. Initially
the beans would be gathered, sorted and dried in the Moluccas,
the original buyers being Malay merchants who paid only for
the trivial cost of native labour in the picking and baling. The
pepper would then be shipped by square-sailed junks to Malacca
on the Malay Peninsula, with many vessels and lives being lost

72

en route through the depredations of Chinese pirates. At Malacca the beans were bought by Hindu traders, who, after paying a heavy tax to the Sultan of Malacca, had to run the gauntlet of further pirates with bases in the Bay of Bengal. The cargoes which eventually got through to the emporium of Calicut were then sold at a handsome profit to Arab traders, who had in addition to pay a tariff to the local potentates. The Arabs would sail for Egypt in convoy, so as to try to beat off the squadrons of Indian *zambucos* which plagued the Arabian coast; but here again many cargoes would be lost.

Once in the Red Sea, the pepper was landed at either Massawa or Jidda. From the former it was escorted by Abyssinian spearmen to the Egyptian border and thence by camel to Alexandria; from the latter it was taken by caravan across the desert to Beirut, successive tributes being paid to the local sheiks and emirs at oases along the route. On either journey losses were heavy. The caravans consisted of relays of some fifty to seventy camels, fastened head to tail by a rope and led by an ass. Grunting and swaying, the 'ships of the desert' would plod along at a sedate two miles an hour, accompanied by a motley rabble of guards. But the gullies and sand dunes of the desert were ideal terrain for an ambush, and the Arabs often found their pepper snatched from them by marauding robbers.

When the caravans reached Alexandria or Beirut, the Sultan of Egypt would collect a full third of the highly-inflated value of its merchandise from the Venetians who came to ship the pepper by galley across the Mediterranean. This final convoy would be menaced by the blockading warships of the Ottoman Turks, by Sallee robbers and by Tripoli corsairs. Even within sight of Venice there were sometimes losses to the Albanian raiders who crept out in small craft by night and boarded the stragglers. The pyramiding of transportation costs and taxes, of gabelle, cumshaw, backsheesh and squeeze, added to the multiplicity of profits on some twelve to fifteen resales between the Moluccas and the markets of Europe, so increased the value of the pepper that a bale of dried beans which had cost one ducat in the Spice Islands would sell in London or Bruges at a hundred ducats: ten thousand per cent of the original price.

It was small wonder that not only the merchants but also the governments of Europe sought a more direct and tax-free route to these fabulous islands of the East. A nation that cornered the trade in pepper would be in a dominating position; an expedition which discovered a quick new route to the pepper-producing islands would enable its sponsors to establish a monopoly which could bring in incalculable wealth. In other words the Portuguese saboteurs who tried to stop Magellan from sailing and the Spanish financiers who tried to divert him from the Philippines, were playing for the richest prize then imaginable.

It would be interesting to know if Magellan was aware of all this. The indications are that he knew very well what the Portuguese were up to and why – several times he wrote to the young King complaining of their machinations, and he went to extreme lengths to supervise personally the loading of all equipment and stores. The duplicity of the Spaniards, on the other hand, seems to have taken him by surprise. He must have grimaced wryly as he saw key positions in his fleet being given to incompetent dandies and the efficiency of his ships' company being reduced by the inclusion of their landlubber retainers, but it can hardly have occurred to him that even before his vessels had left harbour more than half of the captains and *contramaestres* were plotting to kill him and to seize command of his fleet. One reason for his failure to appreciate this may have been that he was too busy to see the wood for the trees. For the commissioning of five ships, 277 men and supplies for two-and-a-half years involved an enormous amount of work. And delegating was not Magellan's forte.

He set up his headquarters on the waterfront at Seville, and here in May 1518 he had his first sight of the five *naos* which had been allotted to him: the *San Antonio*, the *Trinidad*, the *Victoria*, the *Concepción* and the *Santiago*.

We know tantalisingly little about these vessels – as with Columbus's *Santa Maria*, no contemporary drawing of them exists. They had been bought by Juan de Aranda in Cadiz for a total of 1,315,750 maravedis (approximately £1,315: a remarkably small sum even for those days). According to the Portuguese consul, they were 'old and of no great size. And their timbers were rotten and soft as butter. Indeed,' the consul goes on to say, 'I would not care to venture to sea in them, even as far as the Canaries!' This report, however, may well have been a case of wishful thinking; for events were to prove the vessels remarkably seaworthy. The largest was the *San Antonio* (120 tons, cost 330,000 maravedis), then came the *Trinidad* (110 tons, cost 270,000 maravedis), the *Victoria* (90 tons, 300,000 maravedis), the *Concepción* (90 tons, 228,750 maravedis) and finally the

'The duplicity of the Spaniards seems to have taken him by surprise'

74

diminutive *Santiago* (75 tons, 187,000 maravedis). Magellan, in a rare moment of tact, gave the largest vessel to his Spanish second-in-command and hoisted his own flag in the slightly smaller *Trinidad*.

The details of these *naos'* construction and rig is largely a matter of conjecture; but it would seem reasonable to assume they were a cross between Columbus's *Santa Maria* and the graceful high-sterned galleons of the mid-sixteenth century. That is to say, they were three-masted, square-sailed, and had a relatively simple deck structure.

Throughout the summer and autumn of 1518 the vessels were refurbished. Spanish shipwrights had little experience of designing hulls sturdy enough to withstand the crushing waves of the Antarctic; nor did they know how to compensate for the sudden change in temperature experienced by Portuguese East Indiamen as, rounding the Cape of Good Hope, they passed suddenly from tropic to sub-Antarctic seas. The stems, keels and gundecks of the Castilian vessels had therefore to be strengthened; the rotted and worm-eaten timbers were replaced, and the hulls were scoured and re-caulked; new masts were erected, new shrouds and rigging were installed and new sets of top-quality canvas replaced the old.

These were hectic days for Magellan: hectic but happy. For as Parr says:

The Captain General was wholly wrapped up in his work, and at the day's close he found contentment. Comfortably housed in the quarters of Diogo Barbosa, for the first time in his turbulent and straitened life Magellan enjoyed surroundings of elegance and a happy marriage. The charms of Beatriz, the lovely gardens, the fountained courts, and the exquisitely tiled chambers of Alcazar, must have satisfied his pent-up longing for the beautiful side of life. One rejoices that he had that spring and summer in Seville.

In July the King raised him to the rank of Knight Commander of Saint James (the order of Santiago) which did much to enhance his prestige. And to complete his happiness, in the second week of September, Beatriz bore him a son whom they christened Rodrigo.

Indeed Magellan's only real anxiety during this latter part of 1518 was his inability to assemble a suitable crew. There were two problems here. Many of the key positions were filled by order of the *Casa de Antillas*, who, for political reasons, appointed

Following his marriage to Beatriz and his acceptance into the Barbosa family, Magellan lived in luxurious surroundings at the Alcazar Palace pictured here. Exquisitely tiled chambers, elegant gardens and fountained courtyards were the fabric of his new-found fortune.

sycophants rather than seamen, many of whom insisted on bringing with them an unwieldly retinue of retainers. De Cartagena was a case in point; he had no less than eight personal servants, all of whom he expected to lay out his clothes and wait on him at table, but not to haul in the sails or swab the decks. A full sixth of the *San Antonio*'s complement were therefore little better than drones. The second problem was that few ordinary seamen could be persuaded, initially, to sign on. This was partly because the route and destination of the armada was a closely-guarded secret and men were told that they had to enlist blind for a period of 'not less than two years', and partly because Spanish seamen were loth to serve under a Portuguese admiral, and Portuguese seamen were limited (by order of the Council) to a maximum of five per ship. By the spring of 1519 things had reached such an impasse that Magellan felt obliged to write to the King. And the King once again stood by him, tacitly allowing him to ignore the orders of the Council. Magellan therefore at once signed on thirty-seven of his fellow countrymen: able and experienced seafarers who, in the months to come, were to form a professional nucleus aboard each of the five ships.

By the end of May 1519 the armada was to all intents and purposes fully manned. It was not, however, fully loaded with stores; so that although both the King and Magellan were anxious for it to sail, departure had to be postponed again and again. These stores – which the Portuguese made non-stop efforts to pilfer – can be divided into four categories: food and drink, general equipment, armaments and cargo.

The basic food in Magellan's fleet was ship's biscuit, salt beef, salt pork, cheese and dried and salted fish; this was supplemented by anchovies, dried beans and chick peas; while smaller quantities of onions, raisins, figs, nuts, honey, rice, lentils, olive oil and flour were also carried. An extract from the cargo ledger shows the enormous quantities involved:

> 213,800 lb of biscuit
> 72,000 lb of salted beef
> 57,000 lb of salted pork
> 984 lb cheeses
> 5,600 lb of beans
> 10,080 lb of chick peas . . .

The quality of the food provided was good and the quantity generous. The truth is, however, that the diet of *any* sixteenth-

OPPOSITE Vast quantities of
navigational instruments were
taken on the voyage.
Pictured here, lower left,
is a sea astrolabe; dividers for
measuring distances on
the chart; a cross-staff for
measuring celestial altitudes;
a globe; a wooden quadrant
and an hour glass.

century crew was unbalanced, being deficient in green vegetables. It is known today that it is a lack of the ascorbic acid
present in green vegetables which causes scurvy – the disease
responsible for more deaths among seamen than wind, wave
and shipwreck combined. This however was not appreciated
in the sixteenth century; and there is indeed real pathos in the
picture of Magellan painstakingly procuring for his men
'cheeses of none but the best quality' and 'wine of superior
vintage', when in point of fact all that was needed to safeguard
their health was a crate of lemons. As regards drink, we have no
record of the number of water-butts carried; the quantity, however, seems to have been adequate, though the same cannot be
said of the technique of keeping the contents fresh. The wine
consisted of '508 barrels from Jerez' and '417 pipes, 253 butts
and 45 barrels from other sources'. This was enough to provide
each man, initially, with the better part of a watered-down
pint a day.

Apart from food, the holds were filled with a formidable
quantity of what can be best described as material for refurbish-
ing the ships – 'blocks of timber for repairing the hull, standing
and other rigging, six spare sets of best-quality canvas, four
replacement masts, 215 lbs. of nails and [a large but unspecified
quantity of] pitch, tar, resin, tallow and oakum for recaulking
the seams'. Among the larger general items were a forge, an
anvil and a shallow-draught *bergantym* for exploring close inshore; and among the more exotic, $9\frac{1}{2}$ lb of consecrated candles
and 22 lb of beeswax for lubricating crossbows. In addition there
were vast quantities of maps and navigational instruments – '48
parchment charts, 21 wooden quadrants, 7 astrolabes, 24 hour
glasses and 35 compass needles'. The charts were useless. It was
the astrolabes which led them around the world.

The armament of the fleet was also formidable; for Magellan
knew that the Portuguese would not hesitate to waylay him, and
it was essential that his ships be well enough armed to be able
to fight their way out of trouble. An extract from the ordnance
ledger shows the extent of his preparedness:

58 culverins, 7 falconets, 3 large lombards and 3 pasamuros from
    Bilbao
500 lb of gunpowder
Lead-shot, cannon balls of iron and stone
100 corselets, with breast-plates and helmets
60 crossbows, 4,300 arrows and 120 skeins of wire for the bows

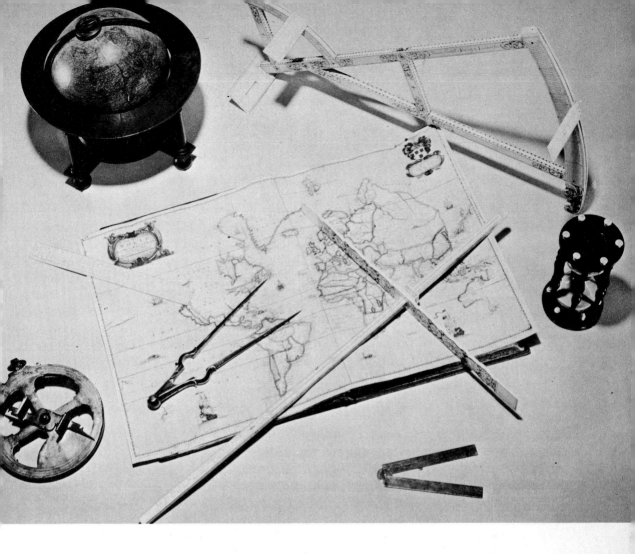

50 arquebuses
200 shields
1,140 darts, 120 javelins, 1,000 lances and 206 pikes

It is sad to relate that the greater part of this armament was used not to defend Magellan against the Portuguese, but after his death to massacre the natives and terrorise the shipping of the south-west Pacific.

Lastly we come to the cargo. And here again the manifest is worth quoting; for the goods listed indicate very clearly the sort of expedition which was envisaged by the *Casa de Antillas* – a trading expedition:

20,000 lb of copper in bars
2,100 lb of quicksilver in flasks

2,000 bracelets of copper and 2,000 bracelets of brass
1,800 small, brightly coloured bells
4,800 cheap German knives
1,000 mirrors, 600 scissors and 1,500 combs
500 lb of crystals, cut into the likeness of jewels
10,000 fishhooks
10,000 bundles of brightly coloured cloth

It can hardly have been a coincidence that this cargo, selected by Cristobal de Haro, was uniquely suited to please the merchants of Malaysia and the Moluccas, nor that the quantity carried would have paid almost exactly for Magellan's five vessels to be laden for their return voyage with pepper.

The assembly and storage of so diverse a cargo was bound to take time, especially as it was hampered at every stage by Portuguese efforts at sabotage. Originally the expedition was scheduled to leave in the autumn of 1518; departure was postponed first to the spring and then to the summer of 1519, and finally Charles lost patience. He ordered the fleet to put to sea on 10 August, whether the vessels were loaded or not. It was the spur the armada needed to get under way.

The day dawned fair and warm, with a welcome breeze dispersing the early morning mist from the valley of the Guadalquivir. As the sun rose, the 277 members of the crew attended a High Mass of farewell in the dockyard church of Santa Maria de la Victoria. There was much pomp and pageantry; much taking, too, of pious oaths. Magellan swore to carry out the King's orders 'with loyalty and dispatch'. The captains and *maestres* swore to 'follow the course of the captain-general and to obey him in all things' – although in truth half of them were already conspiring to kill him. As for the seamen, they took the sacrament cheerfully, little thinking that not one in fifteen of them would see his homeland again. At midday the five ships cast off from the Dock of Mules, their culverins thundered a ceremonial farewell, as the current in mid-river caught them their sails were unfurled and the greatest voyage in history was under way.

It was, however, one thing to order the armada to leave Seville, and another to persuade it to put to sea.

It took the vessels the rest of the day to cover the seventy-five miles to San Lucar de Barrameda at the mouth of the Guadalquivir; here they dropped anchor and set about collecting the last-minute odds and ends which Portuguese pilfering had

'Half of them were already conspiring to kill him'

80

denied them. This took more than a month. Indeed, one gets the impression that no one, except perhaps Magellan, was in any great hurry to leave.

It was during these last-minute preparations that the fleet was joined by its chronicler, a young Venetian nobleman, Ser Antonio Francesco Pigafetta, who had naïvely told King Charles that he was 'desirous of sailing with the expedition so that he might see the wonders of the world'. A more likely motive for Pigafetta joining the armada was that he was a Venetian spy, sent by the Doge to keep track of Spanish trading activities in the East. Be that as it may, his diary is the one contemporary account of Magellan's circumnavigation which has survived, and so we owe this little-known Venetian an incalculable debt, 'for who would Ulysses be without his Homer?'

By mid-September the fleet was at last ready. On the 20th the mistral came moaning down from the hills, the offshore wind for which Magellan had been waiting. He sailed on the ebb-tide. And in the ledgers of the *Casa de Antillas* a clerk made the brief entry: '20 September, 1519. 5 ships and 277 men embarked into the Sea of Mares.'

The sea was calm that night and the moon full. As the land disappeared from sight, slow-burning lanterns were lit and slung from the poops, and the five vessels in line astern went swaying west into the Atlantic. Astrologers had predicted a prosperous voyage.

4 The Atlantic

THE FIRST FEW DAYS out of San Lucar must have been among the most satisfying of Magellan's life. The weather was fine, the sea was calm and the long months of preparing and procrastinating were over. He was at sea at last. His ships' company may still have been uncertain where they were bound – for to quote Pigafetta, 'the Captain-General had omitted to disclose certain particulars of the voyage so as not to alarm the faint-hearted' – but Magellan himself knew exactly the furrow that had to be ploughed; he had promised King Charles that he would discover a new route to the Philippines by sailing west through *el paso*, and he was determined to succeed or perish.

On 26 September the fleet sighted Tenerife, 'a fairy, mist-encompassed island, with the spire of the *Pica de Teide* soaring high into the clouds as though to shipwreck the moon'. The vessels put into Santa Cruz to take aboard last-minute stores: in particular onions, pitch and fresh green vegetables, all of which were cheaper here than in Seville or Cadiz. Tenerife is perhaps the most beautiful of the Fortunate Islands: blue seas and dragon trees; exotic flowers, exotic girls; it must have seemed to the ships' company like a foretaste of the paradise to come. Paradise, however, turned out to have its serpent. The armada had scarcely dropped anchor when a pinnace came racing into harbour, and its captain handed Magellan a letter from Diogo Barbosa. Three of Magellan's captains, this letter said, were plotting to murder him, and Tenerife was the place where they intended to do it.

Forewarned is forearmed, and Magellan in more senses than one kept his head. He knew very well who the captains were – Cartagena of the *San Antonio*, Quesada of the *Concepción* and Mendoza of the *Victoria* – and he deduced that the occasion they would choose would be the conference which he had called for the eve of the fleet's sailing. Sure enough, as soon as the captains and pilots were assembled at this conference, the three conspirators tried to provoke a quarrel, hoping, in the ensuing mêlée, to find an excuse to stab him. Cartagena insisted on sitting at the head of the table; Quesada found fault with the allocation of supplies; and, most provocative of all, Mendoza insisted that when the fleet left Tenerife its course should be not south as Magellan had suggested but south-west. This was stripping the Captain-General of his authority. But to the conspirators' amazement, Magellan meekly gave in, accepting without protest each outrageous demand that they made of

PREVIOUS PAGES On 20 September 1519, Magellan's armada, consisting of ships very similar to these, set sail for the Philippines. Astrologers had predicted a prosperous voyage.

OPPOSITE BELOW The first port of call for Magellan's fleet after leaving Spain was Tenerife in the Canary Islands, where they undoubtedly tapped the indigenous Dragon tree and stored its sap in readiness for their long voyage. The liquor or sap of this tree reputedly held curative qualities ranging from a remedy for dysentery to fastening loose teeth.
OPPOSITE ABOVE The Portuguese are attributed with the discovery of the Dragon tree, first sighted on the Island of Madera (now spelt Madeira), near the Canaries, where it proliferates.

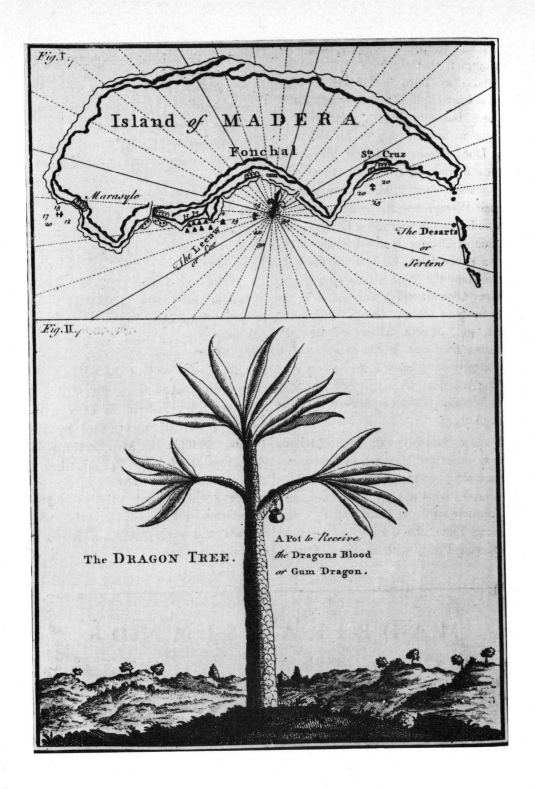

Fig. I.

Island of MADERA

Fonchal

Sta Cruz

Marasylo

The Leenw
or Lee

The Desarts
or
Sertens

Fig. II.

The DRAGON TREE.

A Pot to Receive
the Dragons Blood
or Gum Dragon.

him. The triumvirate were nonplussed; they had not expected such uncharacteristic feebleness. As Cartagena reportedly wrote in his diary: '*El Patituerto* [Clubfoot] showed no spirit. I truly believe that had we spat in his face he would scarce have dared raise a 'kerchief to wipe the spittle away.' Realising, however, that they could hardly strike their commander down in cold blood, the would-be mutineers found themselves balked; and the conference broke up with the Captain-General humiliated but alive. Next morning the five vessels stood into the Atlantic. Their course was south-west.

The winds that October were wayward and the currents perverse, and at the end of a couple of days' drifting and tacking the Canaries were still in sight. The *Trinidad*, all this time, had been in the lead (as laid down in the orders of the *Casa de Antillas*) and now, on the evening of the third day, she suddenly reset her sails and altered course. The *San Antonio* at once luffed under her stern.

'What is your course?' Cartagena shouted to the helmsman. 'South.'

Before Cartagena could protest, the Captain-General appeared on the poop. 'Obey the orders of the *Casa de Antillas*', he shouted. 'Follow the set of my sails by day and my lantern by night.'

Cartagena's hand dropped to his sword. Without doubt he would have liked nothing better than to run the Captain-General through. As it was, divided from him by some hundred feet of water, he could only bawl an undignified protest. The *Trinidad* held her new course, and the *Santiago* (which was also commanded by a Portuguese) immediately followed her. As for the three Spanish vessels, they remained for some minutes rolling indecisively in the swell; then with a bad grace they too fell away to the south. There was much muttering that night among the Spanish captains about the dangers of standing too close to the African coast, but in the morning the vessels picked up both a favourable current and a following wind. Magellan's seamanship had been vindicated, and his authority had been at least partially reimposed.

'It was a discontented fleet that approached the equator'

For several weeks the armada held course to the south, passing between the Cape Verde Islands and the coast of Sierra Leone. The weather was pleasant, with clear skies and a steady wind from astern. Nevertheless it was a discontented fleet which approached the equator. For some owed allegiance to their

86

Spanish captains and some to their Portuguese commander, and who in truth was master no one was sure. It needed a court-martial to bring matters to a head.

The *Victoria*'s boatswain was caught in the act of sodomy, and Magellan ordered a full-dress trial aboard the flagship. As he expected, the three Spanish captains and their aides came armed to the teeth and in belligerent mood, and as soon as the court-martial was over they began once again to taunt the Captain-General, determined this time to force the issue that had eluded them in Santa Cruz. Cartagena was the ringleader. He accused Magellan of hazarding the King's ships by standing too close to the coast of Africa. 'Our course', he said loudly, 'should be boldly into the Maine Sea, not hugging the shore like a ferry-boat.'

But Magellan refused to be provoked. The Spanish captains heaped insult after insult on him, but he offered neither protest nor defence, until Cartagena, determined at all costs to precipitate a showdown, overreached himself: 'No longer', he shouted, 'am I prepared to follow a hazardous course set by a fool.'

It was the act of open defiance for which Magellan had been waiting. He raised his hand, and in a moment the cabin was full of armed men, the *alguacil* and the *Trinidad*'s marines. Gone in a flash was the Captain-General's cloak of meekness. He seized Cartagena by the doublet. 'You refuse in open court to follow my course. Rebel! This is mutiny!'

For a moment Cartagena was numb with shock. Then he lost his head. 'Stab him!' he shouted.

But with the *Trinidad*'s marines breathing down their necks, neither Mendoza nor Quesada was rash enough to reach for his sword. They stood rooted to the spot in dismay while Cartagena was dragged from the cabin, hauled cursing across the deck and clamped like a common seaman into the stocks.

If Magellan had had Cartagena beheaded on the spot he would have been within his rights; however, he considered it more politic merely to strip him of his command and to release him on parole. He must have been tempted to give the captaincy of the *San Antonio* to a Portuguese whom he could trust, but to mollify Fonseca for the degradation of his son he promoted in his place his nephew de Coca. The fleet then continued to the south, the Spanish captains punctilious in following Magellan's course, saluting his flag and reporting each evening for orders. There was no doubting now who was master.

'You refuse in open court to follow my course. Rebel! This is mutiny!'

An impression of St Elmo's fire which is a phosphorescent glow, or a globular light, often visible on the rigging and mastheads of a ship during a storm; it is caused by electrical discharge.

Toward the end of October, as the vessels approached the Equator, they ran into a series of electric storms. For the better part of a fortnight they lay to, doing their best to keep bow into sea. But with their rounded hulls and castellated poops the *naos* were clumsy sailers, and day after day they wallowed gunwale-under, lashed by torrential rain, their decks awash and their yardarms all but feathering the sea. We know that the storms were electric because Pigafetta has left us this vivid if un-scientific description of St Elmo's fire[1]:

[1] Saint Elmo is the patron saint of seamen, and the luminous discharge which glows on masts and rigging during an electric storm was thought in the sixteenth century to be his ghostly presence or 'fire'. No ship's company would ever be lost, the seamen believed, while the saint was with them.

During these tempests the body of St Elmo appeared to us several times. In particular on a night when the sky was especially dark and the storm especially violent, the saint appeared in the guise of a lighted torch at the head of the mainmast; here he remained for more than two hours, a great comfort to us all, for before his arrival we were in despair, expecting death any moment to overtake us. When this holy light was about to leave us, it became so bright to our eyes that we were like blind men calling for mercy. . . . Suddenly the fire vanished and the sea grew calm, and a great multitude of birds settled upon the ship.

They had not settled on it before, presumably, because of the static electricity. This bad weather lasted a fortnight, at the end of which the *naos* were spewed out of the cauldron of storm into the doldrums.

The change was dramatic and, to start with, welcome – no wind, no waves, no rain; the men dried their clothes, sunned themselves on the deck and gave thanks that they were alive. It was only gradually, as day followed airless day, that the truth dawned on them that their armada was becalmed, set fast like flies in amber in a sea as motionless as glass. Magellan had drifted into the Sargasso Sea.

The atmosphere became increasingly oppressive, and the water took on a peculiar sheen, like oiled glass: a sheen composed of millions of microscopic larval eels, on the first stage of their journey to Europe. But though the surface of the sea was motionless, there was a widespaced underwater swell, and the five ships were never still, but spun and pitched this way and that to the groaning of timbers and the rattling of spars. They were athwart the Equator now, and the sun blazed down. The tar melted in their seams, their timbers split open, and the pumps had to be continuously manned – yet so intense was the heat in the hold that after ten minutes' pumping the seamen fainted. Their stores had not been packaged to withstand these conditions; the wheat parched, the meat turned putrid and the hoops of the water- and wine-casks warped and burst.

The crew became enervated; they lolled listlessly in what little shade they could find, grumbling at the shortage of water and cursing the day they had been foolish enough to enlist. On their fourteenth day in the Sargasso the sky began to cloud over. The men eyed the clouds with satisfaction, believing them a harbinger of wind and rain. But alas for their hopes! The clouds brought no wind, and discharged only a tepid shower which

'We were in despair, expecting death any moment to overtake us'

89

Some of the strange creatures of South America as depicted by De Bry in 1596. The figure on the lower right is one of the mythical 'men whose heads do grow beneath their shoulders'.

Granada

I de la Jabaco al trabuguo

Terra d Brea Puerto de los Husspantoles

Trinidad

Punta de la galera

I S Bernardo

in disem flus MACAWINI findet man sill goldi in sand

Di Volcker so an dem Flus ESSEKEBE wohnen kónen in 20 dagen von eingang dises Fluces bis auff einen tagreiß nahe bey den grossen See PARIMÈ schiffen von wanen si alß dan zum ersten ihre Porßiant vnd dar nach ihre Canoas vber landt bis in Obgemelten See dragen ihre hanterung also zu dreiben

KAS dises seind

BALES

MEI

Tigre

MANOÀ oder DORADO dise wirdt geacht fur di grósste Stadt in der ganzen welt

ÆQVINOCTIALIS

IME genant die IAOS aber eillen in der lenge ist ein sich

Ein man des landt IWAI PANOMA ohne kopf

Gestalt der weiber des landis Amazones

Dises Vehe so wier hie verzeichnet haben wt auh andre mehr findet man in GUIANA alle guttes geschm acks auch hatt man hie Hunder Feldhunders Rephunders Cranichs Wachteln Reygers vnd sunst sillerley gefittichs

TISNADA

R de las Amazones

BRASILIÆ PARS

Tabula Geographica nova omnium ... exibens et proponens verissimam descriptionem potentissimi et auriferi Regni GUIANA Sub linea aequinoctiali inter Brasiliam et peru sita per nautam aliquem qui GUALTHERO RALEGH navigatione semper adfuit delineata

Newe landttaffel, in welcher, eigentlich, vnd warhafftiglich fürgestelt wirdt das gewaltige vnd Goldtreiche Künigreich GUIANA so da ligt vnder der Æquinoctial Linien zwischen Brasilien vnd Peru. Observieret vnd abgerissen von einem schiffman so selbst mit her Ralegh der fahrt gewessen

Some of the extraordinary
fauna reputedly sighted by
the Spanish in Brazil.

caused the men's bodies to swell up with prickly heat. The ships
drifted this way and that, flotsam in a stagnating pond.

If Magellan had been becalmed for long in the Sargasso, his
armada might well have perished, for already, after less than
ten weeks at sea, his crew were showing symptoms of scurvy.
But after three weeks a whisper of wind came softly out of the
north; the mainsails of the *naos* came reluctantly to life; blocks
creaked, sheets filled, deflated and filled again, and the armada
with painful slowness began to get under way. The South Equa-
torial Current had drifted them out of the Sargasso into the
periphery of the Trade Winds. By 1 December they were once
again running handsomely under a press of sail, and Magellan
was able to set course for Brazil.

The next month was one of pleasant relief. Magellan knew
that the shores of Brazil were dangerous – the Portuguese had

92

lost many caravels there, and John of Lisbon had expressly warned him of the flat underwater reefs which extended more than seventy miles offshore. When therefore his dead-reckoning plot indicated that he was nearing land, he ordered a round-the-clock watch and took frequent soundings. On 6 December a brightly-coloured land-bird was sighted, and next day the earthy scent of the great Brazilian forests came drifting out of the west. Magellan doubled his watch by day and furled his

On 13 December 1519, the fleet entered what is perhaps the most beautiful anchorage in the word – Rio de Janeiro.

93

sails by night, and at dawn on 8 December a low forested littoral appeared on the horizon. They hit the coast a little south of Cape Roque: a perfect landfall after a voyage of almost five thousand miles. They were, however, in Portuguese waters; a landing would have been impolitic, and the armada therefore followed the coastline south, keeping well out to sea to avoid the reefs. On 13 December they came to an anchorage which was not only beyond the Portuguese sphere of influence but was the most beautiful in the world – Rio de Janeiro.

As luck would have it there had been a drought that summer in Rio; the first rain had not fallen until 12 December, and the natives, the Guarani, looked on Magellan's crew as benevolent

OPPOSITE AND LEFT
Rio seemed to have everything.
At the entrance to the bay
stood Sugar-loaf hill, the
lower slopes carpeted with
exotic flowers. Their time
there was idyllic and after two
weeks of careening and
reprovisioning, the fleet left to
the tears of the natives who
followed them far out to
sea, beseeching them
to come back.

rain-bringing gods. Another aid to good relations was that the *Trinidad*'s pilot, John Lopes Carvalho, had been to Brazil before and was able to speak a few words of Guarani; he could therefore negotiate for food and water and, in due course, for women.

Rio had everything. The scenery was delightful – the fantastic Sugar-loaf hill, the Mediterranean blue of the sea and the emerald green of the forest with its exotic flowers. The food was delightful too – sugarcane, cassava, fresh fish and suckling pig. But the delights most appreciated of all were those of the flesh. For as soon as the Guarani discovered that Magellan's crew were willing to offer such treasures as knives and bells in exchange for a girl, whole bevies of them came swarming aboard. 'They wear', writes Pigafetta, 'no clothes at all except their hair, and in exchange for a knife or an axe we could obtain two or even three of these delightful daughters of Eve, so perfect and well shaped in every way.' For a fortnight there was a saturnalia of feasting and lovemaking; even the priests went ashore, and had to be dragged back to their ships by the *alguacil* and his marines.

Small wonder that the careening and reprovisioning of the *naos* made little progress until Magellan divided the men into two watches and gave them twenty-four hours' leave turn and turn about. Then, in between more important matters, the vessels were beached in pairs, their rotted and storm-damaged timbers were cut out and their keels given a fresh coating of tallow to protect them from the worm they had picked up in the Sargasso. When the ships had been repaired it was the turn of the stores. The foul-smelling butts were emptied, scoured out with vinegar and fire and filled with sweet fresh water;

95

vegetables – yam, cassava, melon and pineapple – were piled high in the holds; and pork was cut into strips, salted and stowed in the empty wine-casks.

Historians have sometimes raised a puritanical eyebrow at Magellan's 'reprehensible activities' in Rio. Yet there was no coercion, no violence, no burning and looting, and none of the frenzied searching for gold which in subsequent expeditions was to lead to such misery and bloodshed. And when, on Christmas morning, Magellan's ships stood south out of Rio bay, the Guarani not only wept but followed them far out to sea, beseeching them to stay. It was quite unlike the departure of most sixteenth-century explorers who left in their wakes a legacy of destruction and fear.

As soon as they were in open water the *naos* crowded on sail; the wind was fresh from astern, the currents were favourable, and for the last few days of 1519 the armada ran free down the coast of South America at the rate of a hundred miles a day. Their butts were full of water, their holds of vegetables and meat, the crew were in good heart and so was Magellan – for he was convinced that he was now rapidly approaching John of Lisbon's strait, the gateway to the East.

And indeed on 11 January 1520 three low hills were sighted on the horizon, which, as Magellan's fleet neared them, converged to form a great south-facing headland, identified as John of Lisbon's Cape Santa Maria. Rounding this, the armada found to their delight a broad reach of water running west-south-west into the sunset as far as the eye could see. They dropped anchor, and Magellan called a conference aboard the flagship. They were now, he told his captain and pilots, approaching seas no Christian man had ever sailed in: on the threshold also of a great discovery.

The fleet split up, Magellan leading some of his vessels south in search of *Terra Australis* (which was shown on all maps as being only a few miles beyond the tip of South America), while Serrano led the diminutive *Santiago* (which had the shallowest draught) westward into *el paso*. Hopes aboard all the vessels must have been high. But it was a gloomy reunion which took place at the end of their searching a few days later. For Magellan had found no sign of *Terra Australis*. And Serrano had found that the westward-reaching seaway was no strait but the mouth of a river.

To say that Serrano's news was a bitter blow for Magellan

would be an understatement. It knocked away the very corner-stone on which his expedition had been conceived; for it negated at a single stroke the inside information that he thought he had gleaned from John of Lisbon's voyages and Martin Behaim's globe. Indeed the news was so bad that Magellan refused at first to believe it. He led his armada west, making slow progress, for the winds were light and contrary, and patches of mist drifted over waters which became increasingly muddy and shallow. The pilots made careful measurement of the tides, and when they found that the flood was becoming ever weaker and the ebb was ever stronger, they knew the worst. Their fears were confirmed when a bucket was lowered over the side and the water hauled up in it was found to be fresh. By the third morning the sea had become so shallow that the fleet was in danger of running aground.

Magellan, however, refused to give in. He lowered the *bergantym*, which had a draught of no more than eighteen inches, and continued doggedly west. But that evening his lookout cried suddenly, 'I see a mountain' – hence the name Montevideo – and as the mist rolled away, the truth was all too clear. Ahead lay not a channel but a great river flowing into a landlocked bay. Their strait was a chimera: their short cut to the Spiceries a myth.

As Magellan called another conference, he must have sensed mutiny with every shift of the wind. And indeed that night aboard the flagship his officers urged him vehemently to make for the Spice Islands by sailing not west, to the unknown, but east via seaways that had been proved navigable and safe; while the representatives of the crew urged him with equal vehemence to return to winter quarters in Rio. But it was now, in his darkest hour, that Magellan rose to full stature. 'We shall go on', he told his assembled ships' companies. 'The strait is not here, but we will surely find it a few miles farther down the coast. We will sail through it, and winter among the islands of the Great South Sea, where even the cooking pots are made of gold and the women surpass those of Rio de Janeiro in beauty.'

This speech has sometimes been quoted as an example of Magellan's duplicity. But it is worth remembering that he probably believed every word he said; for even though *el paso* did not open up round the next headland, he must have felt sure that the southernmost extremity of the continent would. At any rate, though the captains shook their heads and grumbled, the

'Their strait was a chimera: their short cut to the Spiceries a myth'

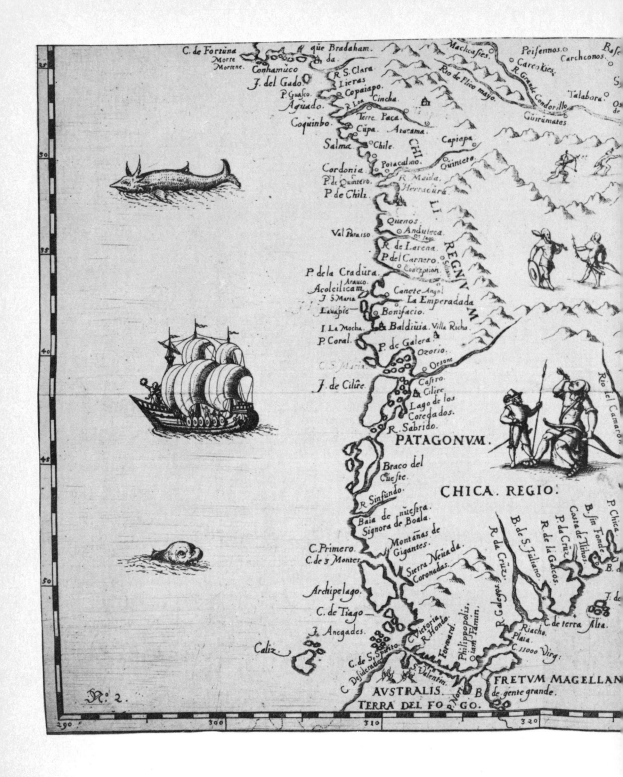

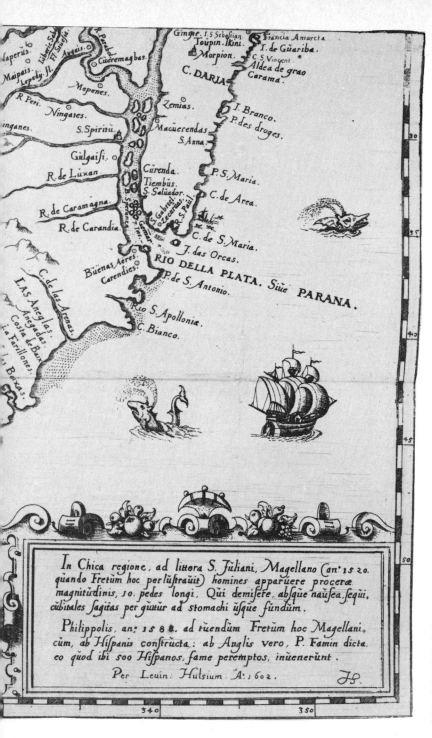

Naperus.
Maipais.
Lepedy. fl.
inganes.
R. Peti.
Ningates.
Mepones.
S. Spiritu.
Gulgaifi.
R. de Luxan.
R. de Caramagna.
R. de Carandia.
C. de las Arenas.
LAS Anegas.
Anegadas.
Costa de Baux.
la Farillones.
Baxas.
Gingie. I. S. Sebastian
Toupin. Ikini.
Morpion.
Francia Antarct.
I. de Guariba.
C. S. Vincent.
Aldea de grao
Carama.
C. DARIA.
Zemias.
Macuerendas.
S. Anna.
Curenda.
Tiembus.
S. Saluador.
S. Gabriel
Zecarius.
R. S. Paul.
C. de S. Maria.
I. das Orcas.
Buenas Aeres.
Carendies.
RIO DELLA PLATA. Siue PARANA.
P. de S. Antonio.
Rio S. Apolloniæ.
C. Bianco.
I. Branco.
P. des droges.
P. S. Maria.
C. de Area.

30

35

40

45

50

In Chica regione, ad littora S. Juliani, Magellano (an° 1520.
quando Fretum hoc perluftrauit) homines apparuere proceræ
magnitudinis, 10. pedes longi. Qui demifere, absque naufea, fequi,
cubitales fagitas per guttur ad stomachi usque fundum.

Philippolis, an: 1582. ad tuendum Fretum hoc Magellani,
cum, ab Hispanis constructa: ab Anglis vero, P. Famin dicta,
eo quod ibi 500 Hispanos, fame peremptos, inuenerunt.

Per Leuin: Hulsium. A: 1602.   HS.

340   350

Magellan was bitterly disappointed when he discovered that the great reach of water just south of Cape Santa Maria was not the hoped-for strait leading to the Pacific Ocean but the estuary of a river – Rio della Plata.

'They were
pioneering seas
no man from Europe
had ever sailed in'

seamen – more loyal, or perhaps more credulous – were won over, and early in February Magellan left the estuary of the River Plate and set course for the unknown and storm-lashed approaches to Cape Horn. From this moment they were pioneering seas no man from Europe had ever sailed in.

To start with, the vessels made good progress, exploring by day every indentation in the coast, and dropping anchor by night in whatever shelter they could find. As they progressed south, however, the seas became steeper and the wind more boisterous; and it was always a headwind, so strong that in the violent squalls which blew up without warning the *naɔs* were driven literally backward. The coast was desolate: bleak headlands and grey steeply-shelving beaches, guarded by reefs and scoured by a thirty-foot tide. It would have been a difficult coast to follow at the best of times, and the armada's progress down it was made more perilous by Magellan's insistence that the ships stand closely into each and every inlet in the hope it would prove the entrance to *el paso*.

For eight weeks the vessels fought their way south, through waters as dangerous as any on earth. They were battered by hurricane winds, bludgeoned by heavy seas, lashed by hail and sleet, and toward the end of their passage weighed down with ice. But Magellan refused to give up. Three times the fleet was scattered; the *Victoria* ran aground, the *Santiago* was dismasted, the *San Antonio* sprang a leak and her pumps had to be manned round the clock; and once in a furious storm the ships were embayed in a gulf where there was no holding ground, and for six days the *naos* were forced to beat to and fro, frantic as swallows ensnared in a windowless room. It was a voyage of appalling hazard, brilliant seamanship and tenacity of the sort that makes history. Modern vessels, in spite of their radar and detailed charts, avoid these waters, which even today are known to local pilots as 'the sea of graves'. For a sixteenth-century sailing ship to have pioneered them for over a thousand miles, at the approach of winter, was a fantastic achievement: an achievement that was due in large measure to the personal skill of Magellan.

For after leaving the estuary of the Plate it was always the *Trinidad* which was in the lead, and nearly always Magellan who piloted her. His was the responsibility of picking a course through the uncharted reefs, sandbars and shoals which lay in seemingly endless succession across their path. For six weeks he was never out of his sodden clothes; for five weeks he never slept for more than a couple of hours at a stretch; and for three weeks he never had a hot meal, for in the near-perpetual blizzards the galley-fires could not be kept alight. In these terrible conditions Magellan was never heard to complain; and his courage and unfailing cheerfulness won him the respect and admiration of his crew. But his captains, as day after day they lurched awk-wardly in the *Trinidad*'s wake, were less charitable in their judgment. 'The fool is leading us to destruction', Cartagena is reported to have cried. 'He is obsessed with his search for el paso. On the flame of his ambition he will crucify us all.'

Cartagena was right. Magellan *was* determined to find the strait or perish; and as his ships reeled south through mountain-ous seas and gale-force winds, with the ice thick on their rigging, the latter alternative must have seemed the more probable.

By the third week of March, however, even Magellan could see that his crew were at the limit of their endurance, and that to have gone on would have been suicide. His captains urged him to give up and to retrace his steps at least as far as the estuary of the Plate. But Magellan remained adamant. 'We shall winter here', he said. 'And in the spring we shall continue our search for *el paso*.'

Wintering in Patagonia, however, was easier said than done; and for day after day the ships reeled on through blinding snow squalls, searching in vain for a harbour. The shore was indes-cribably bleak. For the last six hundred miles they had seen no trace of human beings. And now strange animals 'the like of which no Christian man had e'er set eyes on' began to appear among the offshore rocks. Pigafetta describes them:

> These goslings [penguins] are black and white and have feathers over their whole body of the same size and fashion, and they do not fly, and live on fish. They were so fat that we did not pluck them but skinned them, and they have a beak like a crow's. . . . The sea wolves [fur seals] have a head like that of a calf and small round ears. They have large teeth and no legs, but feet attached to their body resembling a human hand. And they had nails on these feet and skin between the toes like the gosling. And if they could have run they would have been truly fierce and cruel; but they do not leave the water, where they swim wonderously and live on fish.

With such bizarre creatures pacing the *naos* as they staggered south, the crew very likely felt that they were approaching the

'On the flame of his ambition he will crucify us all'

As the fleet headed south
through blinding snow
squalls, searching in vain for
a harbour, they began to
sight strange animals 'the like
of which no Christian man
had e'er set eyes on' – the
Patagonian penguin, seen for
the first time by Europeans.

uttermost ends of the earth. Nor indeed were they far wrong. Eventually, however, on 31 March, the lookout of the *Trinidad* reported a break in the coast. They headed toward it. The entrance was grim, but they stood in boldly, scraping over a foaming bar, and found themselves in the bleak, forbidding but comparatively sheltered harbour of St Julian.

As the armada at last dropped anchor, Magellan must have hoped that his troubles were over. In fact they were about to begin. For the grey cliffs and barren uninhabited shore of St Julian was a very different place from the golden sands and golden girls of the South Sea Islands which the ships' companies had been led to expect. The moment the *naos* were secured, pinnaces began to ply to and fro between the Spanish ships. And soon the thought that for some time had been in many men's hearts was a word on their lips. Mutiny!

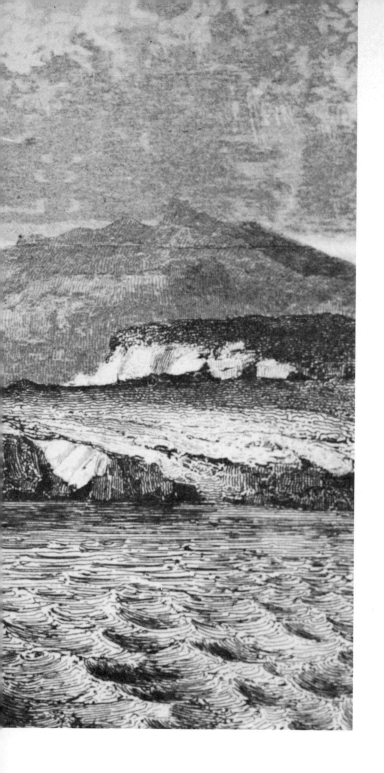

5 Mutiny!

THE EVENTS OF THE NEXT FEW DAYS are recorded, fact-ually and impartially, in Pigafetta's diary. Here is the gist of what he tells us:

Now in this harbour [St Julian] much dissatisfaction and mistrust grew up against Magellan. Immediately after we had dropped anchor, he gave orders for dwellings to be erected on the shore; he also ordered a cut in rations, to ensure that our food supplies would last the winter. The captains and crews objected to both these orders, and the dissatisfied demanded to return home. Magellan refused to discuss the matter, and when some of the crew persisted, he had them arrested and punished. This exasperated the men still further. On 1 April Magellan called everyone ashore for Mass; but the captains Cartagena, Mendoza and Quesada did not appear, and soon afterwards there was open revolt. The ringleader was Cartagena. On the night of 1/2 April he boarded the *San Antonio* [whose captain was loyal to Magellan] and forced her ship's company to acknowledge him as their leader. So on the morning of 2 April Cartagena was in control of three ships – the *San Antonio*, *Victoria* and *Concepción* – and Magellan of only two – the *Trinidad* and the *Santiago*. However, by a cunning ruse, the Admiral managed to win possession of the *Victoria*, and he then placed his three vessels across the mouth of the harbour. During the night fate played into his hands; the *San Antonio* dragged her anchor and came drifting toward the flagship. She was taken with hardly a blow – for on finding themselves boarded the crew quickly declared for Magellan. As a result Cartagena, the next morning, found himself outnumbered and had no option but to submit. The rebels were swiftly punished. Mendoza had been killed during the retaking of the *Victoria*; Cartagena and the chaplain were first put on parole, then (when they again made trouble) marooned, and Quesada was executed. The crew who had taken an active part in the insurrection were condemned to work in chains. . . .

The facts set out above are beyond dispute. Their interpretation, however, is a matter of opinion. For Magellan's admirers argue that the insurrection was due to the jealousy and intrigue of the Spanish captains, while his detractors argue that it was due to the unreasonable hardships he was forcing his ships' company to endure. There is an element of truth in both points of view; and we will not get to the heart of the matter until we understand the relationship that existed between a sixteenth-century captain and his crew.

When historians deal with the occasions on which fifteenth- and sixteenth-century seamen refused to obey their captain, they are prone to condemn the crew's behaviour as mutiny.

PREVIOUS PAGES Pigafetta described St Julian Harbour as desolate and forbidding: a description endorsed by this engraving of the South American coast.

106

The word, however, is inept, and was never used by contemporaries. The Oxford Dictionary defines mutiny as 'the refusal of five or more members of the armed forces to obey the orders of a senior officer'. Sixteenth-century seamen, however, were not members of the armed forces; they were a cosmopolitan rabble scraped together from the waterfronts of half-a-dozen countries, and bound not by King's Rules and Admiralty Instructions but by the far more loosely-framed medieval maritime Laws of Rhodes and Oleron. These laws specifically state that 'a ship's company are entitled to refuse to undertake a voyage which will jeopardise their lives'. And the point is that Magellan *was* jeopardising the lives of his crew; they were therefore within their rights in refusing to follow him, and there is some truth in Zweig's claim that 'justice was on the side of the officers and men. . . . For the punishment he meted out Magellan could have been convicted of murder.'

The events which immediately preceded the 'mutiny' are not altogether clear. Magellan seems to have acted in a high-handed manner in refusing to discuss the men's complaints; on the other hand it was the Spanish captains who triggered off the violence. A little before midnight on Easter Sunday (1 April), thirty armed men, commanded by Cartagena and Quesada, embarked in the *Concepción*'s longboat. Their faces were blackened with charcoal, and their oars 'muffled with the skins of gosling'. It was a moonless night, with fine persistent drizzle, and the longboat drifted down on the *San Antonio* without being seen. A password was whispered, a rope was lowered and the conspirators were hauled aboard. In a matter of seconds they had burst into the captain's cabin and overpowered him. They were just congratulating themselves on a bloodless victory when the *San Antonio*'s boatswain, Juan de Lloriaga, his eyes heavy with sleep, came out of the poop. He was told that no harm would come to him if he kept his mouth shut. Lloriaga, however, was a brave man. 'Ho, *maestre*!' his shout echoed across the water. 'Treason! Arm the men!'

Quesada, beside himself with anger and fear, struck the unarmed boatswain a terrible blow with his sword. But Lloriaga went on crying 'Treason! Treason!' so that Quesada was forced to stab him again and again, six blows in all, till he fell dying across the entrance to the poop. After this, the conspirators met little resistance. Seamen who showed any inclination to remain loyal to Magellan were battened down in the hold; the *San*

'. . . a password was whispered, a rope was lowered and the conspirators were hauled aboard'

Typical dress for a sixteenth-century Spanish gentleman, on land and at sea.
The armed forces had not yet been regimented to the point of wearing uniforms or any specialised form of dress.

Antonio's cannon were trained on the flagship, and the Spanish captains prepared for the second stage of their *coup*, the seizure of Magellan himself.

Had they struck right away they might have succeeded. But they were an incompetent trio, and no seafarers. The currents and tides in St Julian were too fierce for them to dare move against the flagship by night – a sure indication that they lacked the support of the professional seamen in the fleet – so the mutiny therefore hung fire, and at daybreak Magellan was able to make his counter-move. He sent his longboat from ship to ship. The *Victoria*, the *Concepción* and the *San Antonio* fended the longboat off; only the *Santiago* received her loyally, which confirmed Magellan's estimate of his enemies' strength. He struck back with an audacity which took the triumvirate by surprise; and if, in the narrative which follows, he seems to have had more than his share of luck, there is a reason for this: in the last resort, the crew were on his side. (They may have grumbled at the hardships he forced them to endure, but they had sufficient sense to realise they would be far worse off under the landlubbers of Castile.)

During the morning the mutineers concentrated their forces aboard the *San Antonio* and the *Victoria*. It was during this inter-changing of crews that one of their longboats appeared to get into difficulties, being swept by current and tide past the flagship and toward the bar. Her crew were hauled to safety aboard the *Trinidad*, where, under the influence of flattery and wine, they were soon laying bare the facts of the *coup*. Magellan made the most of this piece of good fortune. He ordered the crew whom he had rescued to change clothes with an equal number of the *Trinidad*'s marines, and these marines he then told to re-embark and row slowly past the *Victoria*. At the same time his *alguacil* (Gonzalo de Espinosa) and a couple of un-armed seamen also approached the *Victoria* in a skiff. When challenged, the *alguacil* called out that he had a confidential letter for Captain Mendoza. He was allowed aboard and taken to Mendoza's cabin, where he told the captain that the letter was for his eyes only.

Mendoza does not appear to have been in the least suspicious. When the two men were alone, however, the *alguacil* handed him the letter with one hand and with the other stabbed him flush through the throat with his poniard. Mendoza died instantly; at the same moment the longboat with its disguised crew made a dash for the *Victoria*; the marines came swarming over the side, and before Mendoza's ship's company realised what was happening their captain was dead and their vessel was in Magellan's hands. Espinosa immediately weighed anchor; the *Victoria* drifted toward the flagship; the *Santiago* followed; and before the mutineers' suspicions had been aroused, the entrance to the harbour was blocked by vessels loyal to the Captain-General.

Cartagena and Quesada now showed their lack of fibre. The former meekly begged Magellan for mercy; the latter – who must have realised that he would stand indicted of murder as well as of treason – tried to escape. But the attempt was bungled; before Quesada was ready to move, seamen loyal to Magellan cut the *San Antonio*'s cables, so that she drifted against the flagship. She was captured without loss of life, and the mutiny was over.

There are two sides to every altercation. In defence of the Spanish captains it could be argued that they genuinely believed that Magellan was steering a madman's course and was hazarding the King's ships. They, it should be remembered, owed both their appointment and their allegiance to the *Casa de Antillas*. For them the objective of the expedition was to arrive safely at the Spice Islands, load with pepper and return with a profitable cargo. And they must have felt – not unreasonably – that it was a far cry from the windswept desolation of St Julian to the Elysian Spiceries for which they imagined they were bound. In defence of Magellan and of the reprisals he subsequently took, it could be argued that twice before the Spanish captains had mutinied, and he had forgiven them. On this third and more serious occasion it was no more than natural that he should feel the need both to teach them a lesson and to reassert, in unmistakable terms, his authority.

The trial of the conspirators lasted five days. It was subsequently claimed that Magellan arranged for the evidence to be rigged; but this hardly seems necessary; the facts must surely have spoken for themselves. Early on 7 April the ships' companies were assembled beneath the cliffs encircling the bay. It was a cheerless morning; dark clouds obscured the sky, a chill wind moaned down from the Patagonian plain and in the centre of the beach was an executioner's block. Here Gaspar de Quesada was publicly beheaded, the axe being swung – in return for a pardon – by his foster-brother and secretary Luis

'Dark clouds obscured the sky, a chill wind moaned ... and in the centre of the beach was an executioner's block'

ABOVE On the plateau behind St Julian they encountered the wild llama (guanacos) pictured above. These they killed with their crossbows and cut into strips and salted. The guanacos were described by Pigafetta as having the head and ears of a mule, the neck and body of a camel, the legs of a stag and the tail of a horse.

Before leaving St Julian, Magellan set his ships' companies to work, fishing, hunting and trapping to replenish their supplies. On the mudflats they found shellfish – mussels and crabs; and in the marshes, steamer duck such as the one pictured above.

Molina. His body, and that of the dead Mendoza, was then drawn, quartered and strung up on the gibbets which had been erected at intervals round the bay. Cartagena and the lay priest Sanchez de Reina were sentenced to be marooned. The crew then dispersed – those who had remained loyal to build huts and store-rooms ashore, the mutineers to work for the rest of the winter at careening the *naos* in chains. The gibbets stayed in place for three months, their gruesome remains a reminder that the Captain-General was not a man to be trifled with.

On the off-shore islands Magellan's men found penguins which they bludgeoned to death in their hundreds, salting their flesh, melting down their blubber for lamp-oil, and sewing their pelts into jackets and rugs.

Although St Julian was a grim, claustrophobic anchorage, the loyal members of the armada did not have too bad a time there initially. Their first task was to build cabins in which to sleep and to store the provisions. Wood was plentiful – damaged timbers from the ships, and stunted Nothofagus beech from the lower slopes of the hills – and these, trimmed and interlaced, made massive huts which were proof against even the Patagonian wind. The beech made good firewood too; and fires were soon needed, night and day, for the temperature by mid-April had fallen to well below freezing.

'It was during the unloading of provisions that Magellan made the alarming discovery'

It was during the unloading of provisions that Magellan made the most alarming discovery. Almost half of his victuals appeared to be missing. His first thought was that there must have been petty pilfering during the voyage. It was only when he came to double-check the ledgers that the truth came to light. In spite of his precautions in Seville, almost every consignment had been receipted twice! Portuguese spies had managed to infiltrate the dockyard, and here by bribery had so doctored the books that a bare half of Magellan's provisions had found their way aboard.

A lesser man, with this to contend with on top of the mutiny, would have despaired. Magellan, however, simply set his ships' companies to work, fishing, hunting and trapping, in order to replenish his supplies. On the mudflats of the estuary the men found shell fish in abundance, in particular mussels and crabs; in the marshes they found duck and sea-fowl which they snared or brought down with throwing-sticks; on the offshore islands they found penguins, which they bludgeoned to death in their hundreds, salting their flesh, melting down their blubber for lamp-oil and sewing up their pelts into jackets and rugs; while on the plateau of the hinterland they found herds of 'creatures, passing strange, having the head and ears of a mule, the neck and body of a camel, the legs of a stag and the tail of a horse'; these (guanacos) they killed with their crossbows, cut into strips and salted.

The ship-repairers had a far less pleasant time. The *naos* were careened in pairs. In mid-winter, half-in and half-out of the water this would have been an unenviable task under any circumstances. In chains it was purgatory.

The vessels were beached at high tide and anchored bow and stern. Their cannon were then shifted to one side of the hold, so that the weight of them canted the *nao* onto its side; timbers were inserted as props beneath the hull, and a scaffolding was built along the raised side of the ship. The barnacles and excrescences were then scraped away, and the damaged and worm-rotted timbers cut out and replaced. As soon as the hull had been cleaned and repaired, the seams were recaulked, and boiling tar was poured over the whole of the exposed surface, both to destroy any remaining worm and to afford a protective coating. The ship was then, at high tide, carefully eased on to her opposite beam, and the process repeated. While the *calafate* (caulker) and carpenter supervised this exterior work, the *contramaestre* supervised the less pleasant work on the interior – pumping out and scrubbing down the bilge.

This careening took the better part of three months, and was supervised by Magellan's cousin Alvaro de Mesquita, who proved himself a cruel taskmaster, and earned the undying hatred of the mutineers because he went out of his way to add to rather than to minimise their suffering. So harsh indeed was his regime, that Magellan was forced more than once to intervene to ensure that the men were adequately fed and not taxed beyond the limit of their endurance. Before the winter was out, he ordered Mesquita to strike off their chains.

All this is noted very much *en passant* in Pigafetta's diary, where the mutiny is dismissed in a dozen lines and the reprovisioning and careening in half-a-dozen. What Pigafetta was interested in was the giants.

The Patagonian giants are one of the mysteries of history. There is plenty of evidence that they really did exist. Magellan's men reported them as 'ten spans high', i.e. about seven feet six; two generations later Drake reported them as 'four-and-a-half cubits', i.e. about seven feet four; and subsequent reports describe them as 'at least a head-and-shoulders taller than the average man from Europe'. Yet the present-day inhabitants of this part of the Argentine are small-boned and seldom taller than five feet seven. The giants have vanished, and the only trace of them that remains is the name of their country – Patagonia, land of the big feet. Here is what Pigafetta has to say of them:

We had been two whole months in this harbour [St Julian] without sighting anyone, when one day (quite without warning) we saw on the shore a huge giant, who was naked, and who danced, leaped and sang, all the while throwing sand and dust over his head. Our captain ordered one of the crew to walk towards him, telling this man also to

Also discovered during their stay at the bleak St Julian anchorage were
the Patagonian giants depicted here. Reputedly seven feet six inches
in height – the tallest European reached only midway between their
waist and shoulders.

dance, leap and sing as a sign of friendship. This he did, and led the giant to a place by the shore where the captain was waiting. And when the giant saw us, he marvelled and was afraid, and pointed to the sky, believing we came from heaven. He was so tall that even the largest of us came only to midway between his waist and his shoulder; yet withal he was well proportioned. He had a large face, painted round with red; his eyes were ringed with yellow and in the middle of his cheeks were painted two hearts. He had hardly any hair on his head, what little he had being painted white. . . . The captain ordered him to be given food and drink; then showed him other things, among them a steel mirror. When the giant saw himself in this he was greatly terrified, leaping backwards so that he knocked four of our men to the ground. After this the captain gave him bells, a mirror, a comb and a chaplet of paternosters, and had him escorted back to the place where he had first been seen.

This initial encounter seems to have been friendly enough, as was the second, a few days later, when several families were persuaded aboard:

Our crew made signs to the giants that they should approach the ships. The men came first carrying nothing but their bows; then came the women, laden like asses with a great multitude of goods and chattels. The women were not quite so tall as the men, but somewhat fatter, their faces too were painted yellow and red, and their teats were almost half a cubit long. . . . Our men took eighteen of these giants, both men and women, whom they divided into two parties to help them catch the animals with the body like that of a camel.

Pigafetta goes on to describe the giants' customs and beliefs: how they cured stomach-ache by eating thistles to make themselves vomit, how they cured headache by making great gashes across their forehead, how they lived on raw meat and a root called *capae* and how when they died they believed their bodies were taken over by the devils *Setebos* and *Cheleule*, 'which have horns on their heads, hair down to their feet and who belch fire through their mouth and backside'.

This sort of factual reporting of native customs and beliefs was Pigafetta's forte. In subsequent passages in his diary he gives us similar descriptions of the Alacaluf and the inhabitants of the Marianas and Philippines. These have been proved accurate; we have therefore no reason to disbelieve his stories of the Patagonian giants – especially since he gives us what is obviously an unbiased and painfully truthful account of how Magellan's friendly relations with them were broken.

It appears that Magellan was anxious to take a giant back with him to Spain. His opportunity seemed to come when, early in July, two young males approached the fleet. They were loaded with presents, and were so trusting that when they were offered a pair of fetters they permitted these to be placed round their legs, and not till the bolts were hammered home did they realise they were trapped. 'Then was their fury terrible to behold. They flung themselves this way and that, foaming at the mouth like bulls and calling on *Setebos* to come to their aid. It took a full dozen of our men to restrain them.' Eventually one of the giants indicated by signs that he would come quietly provided his wife was allowed to come too; and the pair of them were therefore taken back to their huts, under escort, to collect their women. The escort was commanded by John Lopes Carvalho, a skilful pilot but a man who was to prove himself time and again a cruel and incompetent bungler. Carvalho first let one of the giants escape; seeing the other struggling to free himself he struck him and seriously wounded him with his sword; he then got himself ambushed. In the confusion which followed, the wounded giant was rescued, one of the escort was killed and Carvalho returned disconsolate to the fleet having lost both his prisoners and done incalculable harm to what had hitherto been a happy relationship.

From this moment the giants regarded Magellan's ships' company with understandable hatred. They took every opportunity of harassing them; they proved themselves formidable antagonists; and their enmity was almost certainly one of the factors which led Magellan, in the height of winter, to seek new quarters. On 17 July he ordered the *Santiago* to make a reconnaissance to the south.

The *Santiago* was the smallest vessel in the fleet, a mere seventy-five tons; and the fact that Magellan let her put to sea in midwinter indicates the faith he had in her commander, John Serrano. Serrano was the oldest of Magellan's captains, and by far the ablest. He needed every ounce of his ability to survive that winter, for no sooner had he cleared the bar than he ran into a series of terrifying storms. So enormous were the waves that the *Santiago*'s waist-deck was continuously submerged; so bitter the cold that if a man touched metal his skin was burned clean away; and so fierce the wind that even the specially-strengthened storm canvas was ripped to shreds.

It took the *Santiago* sixteen days of continuous tacking to

'So enormous were the waves that the *Santiago*'s waist-deck was continuously submerged'

The giants were friendly and persuaded aboard the ships. The women were a little shorter than the men and considerably stouter.

struggle a bare fifty miles to the south. The coast for these fifty miles was desolate: forbidding headlands, grey, steeply-shelving beaches, and low ramparts of grotesquely striated cliff. But on the evening of 5 August they sighted the mouth of an estuary. They stood in next morning, through a skein of shoals, and found themselves in a broad, well-sheltered anchorage. The bottom was sand (and therefore good holding ground), there was wood in the hills, fresh water in the river and an abundance of sea-fowl and fish. And no giants.

Serrano spent the better part of a week recuperating and exploring, then he again put to sea. He may have intended to push even farther south, in which case he would almost certainly have discovered *el paso*, and the Strait of Magellan would be known today as the Strait of Serrano. He may, on the other hand, have intended to return direct to St Julian. In either case he was desperately unlucky. Before he was clear of the estuary, a storm even more violent than its predecessors blew up without warning, and Serrano found himself in the situation that was the nightmare of every sixteenth- and seventeenth-century seaman: embayed on a lee shore.

We can picture the *Santiago* beating desperately to and fro in an effort to gain the comparative safety of the open sea; we can picture her efforts to anchor, and the anchors dragging, and the diminutive *nao* being driven farther and farther back into the shoal water of the estuary. This was a place of death; for where

117

During a reconnaissance to the south of St Julian, the *Santiago*, under the command of John Serrano, became embayed on a lee shore during a storm; she was dismasted, her rudder was torn away and she ran aground on to a sandbar. Theodore de Bry depicts the scene. All but one of Serrano's crew were able to leap to the safety of the shore.

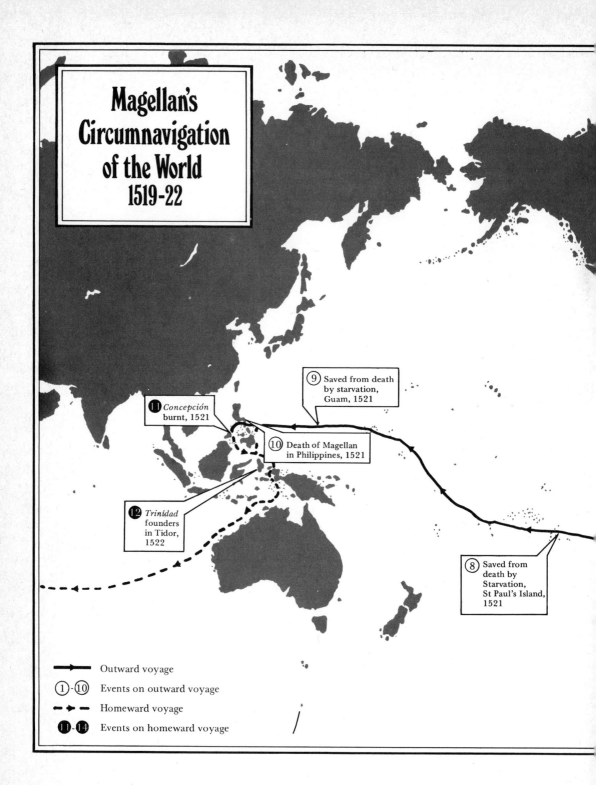

Magellan's Circumnavigation of the World 1519-22

⑨ Saved from death by starvation, Guam, 1521

⑪ *Concepción* burnt, 1521

⑩ Death of Magellan in Philippines, 1521

⑫ *Trinidad* founders in Tidor, 1522

⑧ Saved from death by Starvation, St Paul's Island, 1521

→ Outward voyage

①-⑩ Events on outward voyage

-▶- Homeward voyage

⑪-⑭ Events on homeward voyage

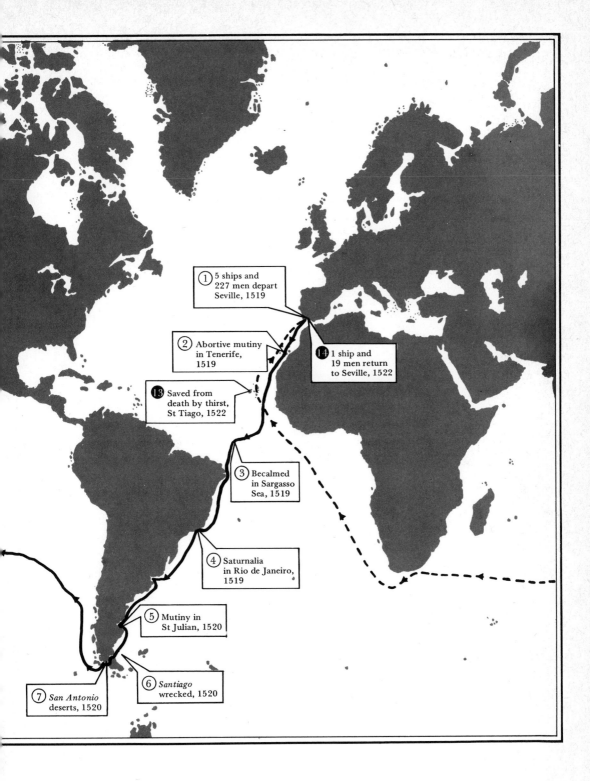

① 5 ships and
227 men depart
Seville, 1519

② Abortive mutiny
in Tenerife,
1519

⑭ 1 ship and
19 men return
to Seville, 1522

⑬ Saved from
death by thirst,
St Tiago, 1522

③ Becalmed
in Sargasso
Sea, 1519

④ Saturnalia
in Rio de Janeiro,
1519

⑤ Mutiny in
St Julian, 1520

⑥ *Santiago*
wrecked, 1520

⑦ *San Antonio*
deserts, 1520

the outgoing river met the incoming tide the surf was steeple-high. The *Santiago* was dismasted; her rudder was torn clean away; but by a superb feat of seamanship Serrano managed to run her aground onto the tail of a sandbar. Here, all her crew except one were able to leap ashore, before the *nao* was sucked off the bar, rolled over and over and whirled away like driftwood into the storm.

Serrano's adventures during the next few weeks have an epic quality in their own right. It was midwinter, and his crew were marooned on a bleak, inhospitable shore with no more than the clothes they stood in. They managed that first night to make a fire from the Nothofagus scrub which grew in profusion at the back of the sand-dunes. Then they built huts, and started to forage for what little food they could find. Two of the crew volunteered to try to walk the sixty-odd miles back along the coast to St Julian. It was a nightmare journey, across rivers, swamps and the ice-bound Patagonian plain; the men had no food except berries and roots, and on the latter part of their trek no water except melted snow. When after eleven days they crawled into Magellan's camp they were so weak and emaciated that their friends failed to recognise them and they were very nearly shot. They managed, however, to gasp out what had happened, and the Captain-General at once sailed south to pick up the survivors.

'The *nao* was sucked off the bar, rolled over and over, and whirled away like driftwood into the storm'

Magellan was so favourably impressed with the estuary Serrano had discovered (that of the Rio Santa Cruz) that he decided to move there for the remainder of the winter, and on 23 August the *naos* were again at sea. St Julian had been a place of suffering, unhappiness and death – fifty years later Drake was also to execute his second-in-command here, literally in the shadow of the gibbets raised by Magellan – and there was widespread relief as the forbidding circle of cliffs disappeared from sight.

Santa Cruz was an anchorage of happier memory. Magellan spent two months there: the days lengthening, the nights losing the worst of their rigour and the crew making great slaughter among the fur seals, whose meat they salted and whose hides they tanned. They also discovered the wreck of the *Santiago* and were able to salvage the greater part of her cargo. By mid-October the armada's casks were full of meat, the butts were full of water, the crew were rested and refreshed and Magellan's thoughts were turning again to *el paso*.

On the eve of their sailing he held a conference. Captains, pilots, officers and the representatives of the men all urged him most vehemently to give up his search for *el paso* and to sail east by seaways which were known till they came to the Spice Islands. 'The Captain', Pigafetta tells us, 'thanked them most courteously for their advice, which he had not the slightest intention of taking.' 'We shall search for *el paso*', he said bluntly, 'until we find it.'

Magellan's authority during the course of the year had become increasingly absolute. His dream now was also, by necessity, the dream of his crew. They were obliged to follow him whether they liked it or not. On 18 October the *naos* were again at sea. They were already closer to Antarctica than any European had been before. And still Magellan's course was south.

6 'El Paso' Discovered

SOUTH OF SANTA CRUZ the coast was even more desolate than to the north. The *naos* explored the mouth of a small river and a number of inlets, but there was no sign of the hoped-for strait. On 21 October they sighted a headland which, since it was the Feast of St Ursula, they named the Cape of the Eleven Thousand Virgins, and rounding this they found themselves in the most magnificent horseshoe bay; the water was a pale aquamarine (and therefore, they assumed, shallow), the beaches were of white sand and in the background, seen dimly through a veil of mist and cloud, was a continuous chain of snow-capped mountains. It was clear to all – except Magellan – that it was no use searching for *el paso* here; nevertheless the *Concepción* and the *San Antonio* were ordered to stand in and explore the centre of the bay. The captains grumbled at such an obvious waste of time, but a sudden and violent storm cut short their dissent and drove them willy-nilly toward the land. The *Trinidad* and the *Victoria* had sufficient leeway to run for the open sea; but the luckless *San Antonio* and *Concepción*, who in obedience to their orders had already stood some distance into the bay, found themselves being swept helplessly toward a daggerlike promontory of rock. Magellan could only watch in despair as the two vessels disappeared into a turmoil of breakers, spindrift and shoals. Nothing, it seemed, could save them from the fate of the *Santiago*.

During the next forty-eight hours, however, the *Victoria* and the *Trinidad* were too concerned with survival to give their consorts more than a passing thought; for as the storm increased in fury they too had to fight for their lives in seas which, as the evening progressed, took on a terrifying malevolence. Soon huge waves, a mile and a quarter from crest to crest, were thundering in endless succession out of the south; each as it neared the *naos* towered high over their masts and seemed certain to engulf them. Yet somehow the labouring vessels always managed to rise, to hang trembling for a moment on the spume-driven crest, then plunge down and everlastingly down into the maw of the following trough. Their hatches and gun-ports were stove in; their pumps had to be continuously manned; the *Victoria* was dismasted; several times the *Trinidad* rolled to within an ace of turning turtle; men were swept overboard; yet somehow both vessels managed to stay afloat, and forty-eight hours later they came clawing back past the Cape of the Eleven Thousand Virgins into the horseshoe bay.

126

There was no sign of the *Concepción* and the *San Antonio*.

Magellan must have been close to despair. He had already lost one ship; the disappearance of two more was a crippling blow, and of the hundred-odd men who were missing, Mesquita (captain of the *San Antonio*) was his kinsman, and Serrano (who had recently been made captain of the *Concepción*) his closest friend. He scanned the shore section by section hoping desperately for evidence of survivors; but there was not the slightest indication of life.

Next morning, as soon as it was light, the two *naos* headed into the bay, making for the rocky promontory behind which their companions had disappeared. To start with there was no movement, apart from a handful of high-flying gulls; but as the *Trinidad* neared the shore her lookout gave a sudden cry: 'Smoke!'

For a moment all eyes were on the column of white, suspended pencil-thin between mountains and sky. Then, as the *Trinidad* rounded the tip of the promontory, her crew caught their breath in amazement. For there in front of them – quite hidden from the open sea – lay a deep-water strait: and a strait which this time gave no indication of petering out, but ran westward through the encircling mountains as far as the eye could see.

They had barely recovered from their surprise when the lookout gave another cry. 'Two sail! Closing fast.'

There was a rush for the bow. Soon the crew could make out a pair of *naos* running free towards them under a great press of canvas. It was the *San Antonio* and the *Concepción*. And as they neared the flagship, Magellan saw they were bedecked with pennants and flags, and that men were waving, shouting and rolling in abandon about their decks; and it came to him in a moment of pure, unadulterated joy that not only had his missing ships been restored to him, they had discovered *el paso*.

The *naos* dropped anchor, while the discoverers boarded the flagship to report. All was smiles, *bonhomie* and congratulations now, with the captains and pilots as vociferous in Magellan's praise as a few days earlier they had been in his condemnation. Here is Parr's account of the report they brought back:

After exhausting every manœuvre to escape the lee shore, the two ships had been swept round the promontory and blown helplessly toward the breakers. Suddenly they saw a narrow passage, like the

'Magellan saw they were bedecked with pennants and flags . . . they had discovered *el paso*'

127

mouth of a river, ahead of them in the surf, and managed to steer into it. Driven on by wind and tide, they raced through this passage and into a wide lake. Still driven by the storm they were carried west for some hours across this lake into another narrow passage, though now the current had reversed, so that what appeared to be a great ebb tide came rushing toward them. They debouched from this second strait into a broad body of water which stretched as far as the eye could see toward the setting sun. Excited and triumphant, they crossed this to where it discharged into several west-reaching channels. They entered one of these, and observed that it bore the marks of a 40 foot tidal drop along its precipitous shores. Taught by their previous disillusion when they had assumed the Rio de Solis to be el paso they made continuous tests of the water to see if its saltiness decreased as they left the Atlantic; they found, however, that it continued to be brine throughout. Another lesson which they had learned was to check the comparative flow of the ebb and flood tides to see if the former became stronger, as it would if augmented by the flow of a river; their observations, however, showed that the tides were equally strong; hence they assumed that there must be an outlet to the west. Frequent soundings indicated a deep channel without sandbars or shallows, and every test and check convinced the pilots that this was indeed a genuine strait which opened up into a great body of water – almost certainly the Great South Sea. They seized on a change of wind to race back to Magellan with the news.

To say that the Captain-General was elated would be an understatement. Some of his pilots, however – in particular Estevan Gomes of the *San Antonio* – still advocated that they return by an easterly route to the Moluccas. 'With provisions for a bare two months,' he argued, 'it would be madness to head into the unknown.'

Magellan, however, believing that his goal was to all intents and purposes virtually in sight, was in no mood to turn back. 'Though we have nothing to eat', he cried, 'but the leather wrapping from our masts, we shall go on!' Gomes was outvoted, and the fleet stood west into *el paso*.

Their voyage to start with was pleasant enough, the narrows opening out to form a stretch of sheltered water surrounded by hills. It was while they were crossing this that they sighted more smoke, and a little later what looked like a native village. Magellan sent a landing party ashore; but all they found was a dead whale, stranded at the water's edge like the great grey hulk of a ship, and a few hundred yards inland a circle of burial platforms. On these platforms they found 'bodies of the

OPPOSITE A sixteenth-century map of South America. It illustrates the belief that the Strait of Magellan was a narrow passage between two large land masses. Note the Patagonian giants and the exaggerated size of the River Plate.

128

Mare antiliarum.
SEPTENTRIO
Peru.
America
Mare aque dulcis
EQUINOCTIALIS
Cambales.
Brasilus.
Quarta orbis pars.
TROPICUS CAPRICORNI
Terra argẽtea.
Mundus novus.
Terra Incognita
ORIENS
Mare muẽtũ p magalhões.

Pathagoni, each a full seven feet tall; at his side a spear, a club studded with shark's teeth and several small pieces of iron ore and flint'. It was an eerie scene: grey sky, bare landscape and the huts creaking and rustling under a bludgeoning wind. The landing party blessed themselves, and beat a hasty retreat to their vessels.

As the fleet continued westward, the country on either side of *el paso* became more spectacular. The hills gave way to mountains, and the pampas to forests of beech and pine. Eventually they came to a narrow defile, where the walls were precipitous, and currents and tide rips tore great whirlpools out of the sea. Magellan's skill as a pilot was tested to the full; but with the aid of a slack tide and a following wind he managed to lead his armada safely through. They then emerged into a more placid body of water, 'like a great lake surrounded by snow-capped mountains'. And here there took place an incident of some ambiguity: the loss of the *San Antonio*.

There was, it seems, a large island in the middle of the 'lake'. The *Trinidad, Victoria* and *Concepción* passed to the north of it; and Magellan ordered Mesquita in the *San Antonio* to reconnoitre to the south and to rejoin him within forty-eight hours. He can have had no premonition as the *nao* swung out of line that he was never to see her again.

It took the armada the better part of two days to cross the 'lake', at the end of which they came to a narrow channel running dead straight to the west-north-west between over-hanging walls of rock. It was an awe-inspiring place; for the cliffs rose sheer to over a thousand feet, and the currents zig-zagged this way and that like ink spilt into the sea; while to add to Magellan's troubles there was nowhere to anchor and no sign of the *San Antonio*. He decided to search for a place where his vessels could be moored and, while they waited here for the *San Antonio*, to probe the channel by *bergantym*. Eventually a suitable place was found – a small inlet which they named the Creek of Sardines, since it was full of darting quicksilver fish. The *bergantym* was assembled that evening, 30 October, and the next day it set off down-channel under the command of Espinosa.

The entry in Pigafetta's diary is brief, and has none of the sense of occasion which one might have expected him to feel when chronicling one of the great moments in the history of exploration. He says simply:

'... as the *Trinidad* rounded the tip of the promontory, her crew caught their breath in amazement. There in front of them lay a deep-water strait: and a strait which this time gave no indication of petering out, but ran westward through the encircling mountains as far as the eye could see.

RIGHT Contemporary
portrait of Magellan by an
unidentified artist.

BELOW This map, drawn
soon after Magellan dis-
covered the route from the
Atlantic Ocean to the
Pacific in 1520, shows the
early misconception of the
Strait as a clear, open
passage. In fact, the actual
Strait is a series of narrow,
twisting channels between
islands and the tip of the
South American continent.

Soon after [reaching the Creek of Sardines] we sent a boat well equipped with men and provisions to search for the entrance to the other sea. They spent three days going and returning, and when they got back they told us that they had found the entrance and had seen beyond it the great and wide ocean. Whereat the Captain-General, for the joy that he felt, began to weep and said that the headland at the mouth of the entrance should be known as Cape Deseado, as a thing much desired and long sought.

From these bare bones Parr has fashioned a more vivid reconstruction of Espinosa's discovery:

After leaving the Creek of Sardines he passed down the strait, a bleak and desolate waterway cleft between barren shores which were made up of riven rocks piled one on top of another by volcanic and seismic convulsions. There were no suitable beaches on which to spend the night, no safe anchorage, and the crew had to pass three nights in the cramped and open boat exposed to incessant rain. The winds were tempestuous, continually shifting, so that the bergantym was almost driven several times against the rocks. The 40 foot tides rushing westward met the immense Pacific swell rolling eastward; this caused a confused and turbulent sea, and when the great waves dashed against the cliffs they created backwashes which added to the confusion of the waters. . . . Along one side of the strait a strong current flowed east; along the opposite shore an equally strong current flowed west; where the two met there were whirlpools and fierce eddies. None of the seamen had ever before experienced such conflicting and hazardous currents.

To add to their troubles, when they came at last to the end of the channel and saw ahead of them the open sea, an unexpected current nearly swept them to certain death among the giant rollers of the Pacific. It was only the *alguacil*'s presence of mind that enabled them to pick up an east-flowing tide rip which bore them back to the comparative safety of *el paso*. As they rested panting on their oars the Great South Sea and the islands which lay scattered across its approaches disappeared in a squall of torrential rain. But they had seen enough: an approach route to the greatest ocean on earth.

On returning to Magellan, the crew of the *bergantym* were given a heroes' welcome. But there occurred soon afterwards an incident which seems, unaccountably, to have made a greater impression on contemporary chroniclers than the epoch-making voyage of the longboat: the affair of the vanishing Indians.

Theodore de Bry's map of the newly discovered Strait. He decorated it with Patagonian giants and some of the creatures allegedly discovered by the ships' companies.

One evening a little before sunset the *Trinidad's* lookout reported the approach of two canoes. The *naos* were moored in the Creek of Sardines at the time, close under a small cliff, and were invisible from the main strait; it was not therefore till the canoes had actually entered the creek that their occupants saw the armada. There was no doubting their consternation. They dropped their paddles and stared open-mouthed at the great vessels, the like of which they had obviously never seen in their

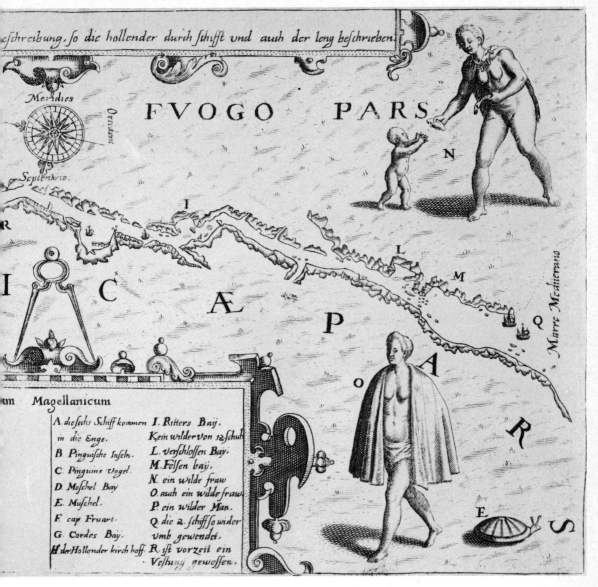

FVOGO PARS

Meridies

Oriental

Septentrio

I

R

I C Æ

P

A

R

S

Marre Mediterano

N

L

M

Q

O

E

Magellanicum

A. dieſechs Schiff kommen I. Ritters Baij.
  in die Enge.   Kein wilder von 12. ſchul
B. Pinguiſche Inſeln.   L. verſchloſſen Bay.
C. Pinguins vogel.   M. Felſen baij.
D. Moſchel Bay   N. ein wilde fraw
E. Muſchel.   O. auch ein wilde fraw
F. cap Fruart.   P. ein wilder Man.
G. Cordes Bay.   Q. die 2. ſchiff ſo wider
H. der Hollender kirch hoff vmb gewendet.
                         R. iſt vorzeit ein
                          Veſtung geweſſen.

lives. For several seconds they seemed powerless to move; then they fell to their knees, burying their faces under the gunwale and stretching out their arms as though in supplication – a gesture which their descendants were to emulate, down to the last detail, first with Cook and subsequently with Darwin.

Magellan ordered the *bergantym* to tow them alongside, and the seamen in charge prudently gathered up their harpoons and knives before bringing them aboard. They numbered about a dozen, men, women and children in equal number. They were, Pigafetta tells us, 'stalwart savages, upright and powerfully built, though nothing like so tall as the Pathagoni'. They were naked except for an evil-smelling sealskin between their legs, and their bodies glistened with a sheen of fish oil which protected them so effectively from the cold that when one of the women suckled her child she did not bother to brush the snow from her naked breast. Magellan gave them bells, combs and a mirror, none of which they seemed to know what to do with; when, however, he gave them raw meat they devoured it ravenously. Carvalho, Black Henry and Pigafetta all tried to talk to them, but could make themselves understood only by mime.

Soon it was dark. The natives, however, showed no inclination to leave. When they felt tired they simply lay down on the deck and within minutes were asleep, the mist forming a fine frozen veneer of white on their naked bodies. Magellan ordered their canoes to be hoist aboard and their weapons to be piled up in the waist-deck; he also ordered the seamen on watch to keep an eye on them during the night. The seamen swore that they heard no sound and saw no movement. But at sunrise the natives had vanished together with their weapons and canoes. 'And the superstitious crossed themselves and said they had known all the time that they were spirits.'

A few days later the fleet stood out from the Creek of Sardines. Their course, however, was east rather than west; for there was still no sign of the *San Antonio*, and Magellan had decided to retrace his tracks in an effort to find her. He searched for her for the better part of three weeks: firing cannon, lighting bonfires and probing deep into the tortuous maze of channels. Several times in the violent tide rips his *naos* came within a hairsbreadth of being wrecked. But they could find no trace of the missing ship. Like the Indians, she had vanished as though she had never been. Magellan thought that she might perhaps have been blown back into the Atlantic. But the fleet astrologer made a more realistic prognostication; there had, he declared, been a mutiny; Mesquita had been wounded and taken prisoner; and the *San Antonio*, under the command of Estevan Gomes, was on her way back to Spain.

There are two reasons why Magellan tried so hard to locate the *San Antonio*. Firstly, her captain was his kinsman; and although Mesquita may have been neither an attractive

Contemporary chroniclers made much of the incident of the vanishing Indians of *Tierra del Fuego*. In spite of being guarded during the night as they slept aboard the *Trinidad*, by morning they had disappeared, no one having seen or heard them go!

RIGHT Before setting off on his voyage across the Pacific, Magellan had gathered abundant but ill-chosen provisions, thus, unwittingly exposing his men to the ravages of scurvy. Almost nothing was known of the causes of this dreaded disease. Anti-scorbutic plants, such as this *Apium Antarticum* which abounds in the Strait of Magellan, would have safeguarded the health of Magellan's men.

OPPOSITE These marine animals – molluscs, a tunicate (centre) and crustaceans (top right) – abound in the waters around the Strait of Magellan. Although not anti-scorbutic, a steady diet of these creatures would have kept many more of Magellan's men alive, had they but known of their existence and dietetic qualities.

apium antarticum.

138

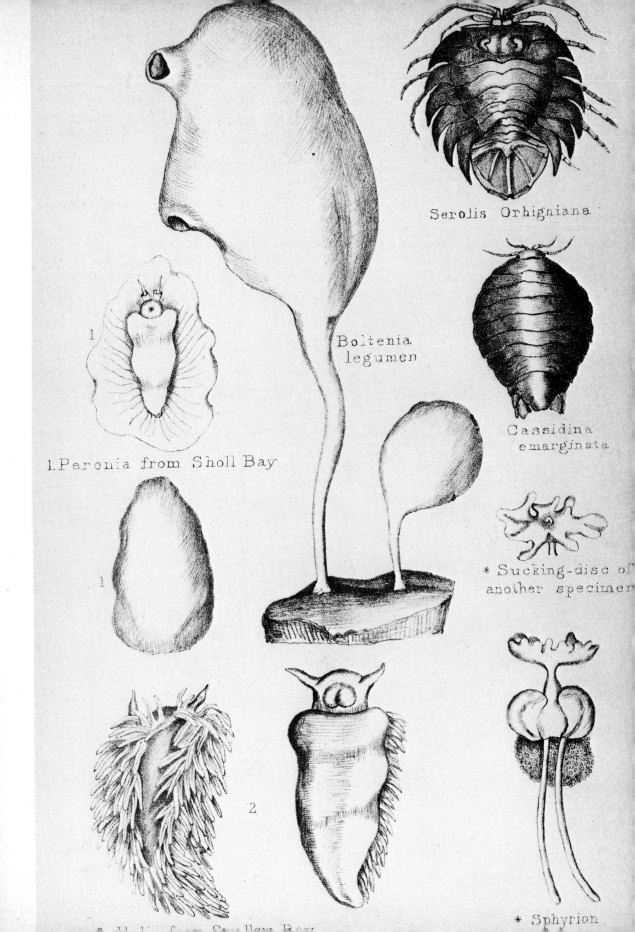

Serolis Orhigniana

Boltenia legumen

Cassidina emarginata

1. Peronia from Sholl Bay

1

* Sucking-disc of another specimen

2

* Sphyrion

character nor an able commander, Magellan was almost obsessively loyal to his kith and kin. Secondly, the *San Antonio* had made off with the greater part of the fleet's provisions. When in mid-November, Magellan made an inventory of the food which was left he was appalled. For the *San Antonio* – the largest and therefore it had been assumed the safest ship in the fleet – had had in her hold a third of the armada's biscuit, a third of its meat and almost two thirds of its currants, chick peas and figs. When the captains and pilots learned the situation they urged Magellan yet again, with all their eloquence, to give up the idea of further exploration. But the sights of the Captain-General were firmly fixed on the Philippines. He put the officers on oath not to disclose that the fleet was desperately short of provisions, and put the men to work hunting and fishing.

The provisions they collected were abundant but ill-chosen. Scurvy would be their greatest threat, and the Strait of Magellan abounds in antiscorbutics – 'nutritious sea kale', 'wild celery as good as any I have tasted' and 'whole banks of the very sweet herb called *Appio*' – yet Magellan collected none of these. He concentrated exclusively on restocking his larder with fish and meat: on seining sardines, snaring sea-fowl and shooting rabbits, cavies and prairie hens; he even encouraged Espinosa to take a hunting party ashore in search of guanacos and rheas. The green vegetables which were his for the taking, he disregarded – as subsequent explorers were, in their ignorance, to disregard them for the better part of 250 years. In this lay the seeds of tragedy.

On 26 November the three *naos* headed west down the last few miles of the strait. They sighted no more Indians. But at night the land to the south was dotted with camp fires, which led Magellan to christen it *Tierra de los Fuegos* (Land of the Fires).

On 27 November they came to the open sea. It was a stormy evening, typical of the approaches to Cape Horn: a bludgeoning thirty-knot wind, majestic wide-spaced waves and long spells of driving rain interspersed with short bursts of brilliant sun. The armada spent the night in what little shelter they could find, and at daybreak stood out to sea.

For a couple of hours the *naos* pitched and rolled and spun and swooped at the mercy of the sea; for where the incoming rollers met the outgoing tide the seas were knocked up into as wicked a mill race as any the fleet had sailed through. By

An hourglass was important to early mariners as mechanical clocks were unreliable at sea. Time measurement was an important element in 'dead reckoning' navigation by which the early pilot worked out the ship's position.

RIGHT During the latter stages of the voyage down the strait numerous camp fires were sighted on the southern shore which led Magellan to name the area *Tierra de los Fuegos*, Land of the Fires. This was subsequently altered to the Spanish *Tierra del Fuego*.

BELOW Images of the inhabitants of Magellan's *Tierra de los Fuegos*.

midday, however, they were in calmer waters, the sun as if to greet them broke through the banks of cloud and Magellan signalled the *Victoria* and the *Concepción* to close.

It was a solemn occasion. The crew were paraded on deck, and Father Valderrama (the most senior of the priests) climbed on to the flagship's poop. The ships' companies knelt in prayer as he invoked the grace of Our Lady of Victory; they sang the *Te Deum*, their voices small and insignificant in the wind; then the carronades thundered a broadside, and the sea birds scattered in fright. Before the crew were dismissed, Magellan unfurled the lions and castles of Castile. 'We are about to stand into an ocean where no ship has ever sailed before', he cried. 'May the ocean be always as calm and benevolent as it is today. In this hope I name it the *Mar Pacifico*.'

The armada stood west. The hopes of the ships' companies were high that evening, for they expected that in three or four days at the most the longed-for Spice Islands would be sighted over the horizon. It is merciful that the truth was hidden from them: that less than half of those aboard would live to see the islands for which they had already sailed halfway across the world.

LEFT Painting on the ceiling of a church at Cebu in the Philippines, depicting Magellan planting a cross and commemorating the first Christian baptism on the island.

7 The Pacific

MAGELLAN'S FIRST FEW WEEKS in the Pacific were uneventful. To start with, the armada stood north, running
parallel to the coast of Chile. After a couple of days they picked
up a current from astern (the Peruvian Drift) and a wind from
abeam (the Westerlies); the sea became progressively calmer
and the climate balmier, and as they approached sub-tropical
waters there was a welcome increase in the number of sea birds
and fish.

These were lazy, peaceful days, with the crew congregating
in the lee of the foc's'le and, in their innocence, working out the
value of the spices which they expected any day to be loading.
Indeed the whole of December was so lacking in incident that
Pigafetta in his diary devotes only some dozen lines to it, most
of which consist of a passage describing 'a very amusing hunt of
Fishes':

There are in this ocean three sorts of fish, a cubit or more in length,
which are named Dorades, Albacores and Bonita. These follow and
hunt another kind of fish which flies and which we called Colondriny

PREVIOUS PAGES Magellan's
men reported the strange
phenomenon of flying fish,
which led European artists to
paint imaginary pictures of
schools of fish leaping in
great bounds out of the water.
From *India Orientalis*, 1598.

BELOW The ships companies
observed many species of fish
when they entered the Pacific.
This highly colourful variety
they named Dorades.
They also found Albacores
and Bonita.

148

[sea swallows], a foot in length and very good to eat. And when the three kinds of fish find the Colondriny in the water they chase them and make them fly – and they fly for as long as their wings are wet, about the distance a man can fire a crossbolt. And while the Colondriny fly, the other fish swim after them, seeing and following their shadow; so that as soon as they re-enter the water they attempt to seize and devour them – a merry and marvellous thing to see!

Feeling perhaps that the predators should not have it all their own way, the crew also took to fishing, baiting their lines with streamers of rag to make them look like the Colondriny. These they lowered from the bowsprit; and soon bonita and albacore were making a welcome addition to their diet.

So the weeks drifted by: each day a steady wind, a cloudless sky and a sun that grew steadily warmer; each night the bows of the *naos* cutting a swathe of phosphorescence out of a quiet sea, and their masts swaying slowly across a backdrop of unfamiliar stars. There was neither danger, discovery nor discontent. The crew's worst enemy was boredom.

About the middle of the month Magellan altered course to the west-north-west. He was nearing the thirtieth parallel now, and expecting any moment to sight the coastline of Asia. But day followed uneventful day and there was still no sign of land. Gradually first the birds and then the fish were left astern. And by the end of the month the *naos* were alone: alone, that is, except for the handful of black triangular fins which continued, as if in anticipation, to circle their wake.

Although he had no means of knowing this, Magellan had picked an unfortunate course. If he had headed west, after crossing the thirtieth parallel, he would have sighted the

Squal. Carcharias _ *White Shark.*

Also sighted by the crew was the white shark, schools of which circled menacingly week after week in their wake.

Tuamotu or the Society Islands, which lie scattered across 300,000 square miles of ocean. As it was, his course of west-north-west took him a shade to the north of these archipelagos, and into the empty reaches of the central Pacific. Islands here were few and far between, and the masts of Magellan's ships were not sufficiently high for his lookout to be able to see more than four or five miles in any direction. Unless therefore they happened to be heading directly toward an island, they had little chance of sighting it. Nor was their navigational knowledge sufficiently advanced for them to have the slightest idea of how far to the west their goal lay. All they could do was to arrive at roughly the right latitude, and continue to sail blindly on.

Magellan depended for his navigation principally on three instruments: the astrolabe (or cross-staff), the compass and the hourglass.

The astronomer's astrolabe was a delicate and elaborate piece of equipment, ill-suited for use on the heaving deck of a ship; but its simplified seaman's version, the cross-staff, was accurate enough to calculate a reasonably precise latitude. It consisted of a boxwood rod about three feet long, one side being graduated in degrees and minutes. One end of it was held to the eye, while a cross-piece at right-angles to the main rod was moved up and down till its position corresponded to the distance between horizon and Pole Star; the altitude was then read off from the scale. On a calm night with good visibility this cross-staff was accurate to within a degree of latitude.

The compass was kept in a special *bitácula* (or little dwelling), a wooden box which was illuminated at night by an oil-burning lantern. This compass was often known as the Stella Maris – a name subsequently transferred to the Pole Star itself. The monk Felix Faber has left us a good description of how it was used:

They have one Stella Maris near the mast, and a second on top of the poop. Beside them all night burns a lantern. There is a man who constantly watches the compass card and never once takes his eye off it. He gives directions to the man at the tiller, telling him how to move the bar. And this man dare not move the helm in the slightest degree except at the orders of him who watches the Stella Maris.

The actual needle of this compass featured in many a foc's'le yarn: if placed under the pillow of an adulterous wife it was said to make her confess, while the seamen claimed it was a cure for venereal disease.

The hourglass was the ship's only timepiece; it was also an instrument of navigation in its own right. The sole method of calculating longitude in Magellan's day was by dead reckoning plot: i.e. by laying off a vessel's track from a known starting point, day after day, onto a chart. To do this a navigator needed to know his course (which he could tell from his compass), his speed (which he estimated by tossing a bit of wood overboard and seeing how long it took to disappear) and the time for which he had been travelling (which he could tell from his hourglass). This glass was usually kept in the same *bitácula* as the compass. The most junior of the seamen had the job of looking after it, reversing it every couple of hours when the sand had run through, and ending his watch by singing the ditty

> The watch is changed,
>   The Glass is running.
> We shall have a good voyage
>   If God is willing.

If a man was caught 'warming the glass' by holding it against the lantern or under his shirt he was flogged, for when the glass was warm it expanded, the sand ran through more quickly and the tedious spell of duty was shortened; but at the same time the ship's timekeeping and hence her navigation was placed in jeopardy.

With the aid of these instruments Magellan had, by Christmas 1520, led his armada into the approximate latitude of the Moluccas – ten degrees south. He must have reckoned that if he headed west-north-west he was bound sooner or later to

151

RIGHT A woodcut of 1557 showing sailors taking readings using an astrolabe and the traditional cross-staff.

BELOW A nocturnal made by Humphrey Cole in 1580. An elaborate form of what is basically a simple device for telling the time of night by the relative positions of the 'guards' of the Pole Star on any day of the year.

ABOVE An early sixteenth-century engraving by Stradanus of a contemporary cosmographer in his study. His instruments include compass, dividers, rule, quadrant, sand-glass, armillary sphere and, in the left foreground, a lodestone.

LEFT A cross-staff made by Walter Arsenius at Louvain, *c.* 1571. An arm-aching, eye-blinding method of measuring celestial altitude.

reach either these islands or the Philippines, which lay slightly northward of them. It was a logical calculation. But it failed to take into account the factor which neither Magellan nor anyone else suspected – the vastness of the Pacific.

Their passage to start with was more monotonous than hazardous – with the south-east Trades a steady fifteen knots from their quarter, the crew had no need even to raise or lower sail. After a while, however, the loneliness of the Pacific began to make itself felt. As the *naos* forged ahead for week after week with never a sight of land, the crew became anxious – Atlantic voyages had never lacked a landfall as long as this. The monotony began to fray their nerves: day after day the same blustering wind from their port quarter, the same unclouded sky, the same blazing sun and soon the same hunger – for Magellan, alarmed at their failure to make a landfall, ordered a cut in rations.

But worse was to come. For as they stood deeper into the tropics, the little food they had began to deteriorate. Their penguin and seal meat was the first to go. Under the burning sun of the Equator it turned putrid, breeding long white maggots which crawled everywhere and ate, with impartial voracity, clothes, leather, timbers and supplies. The water in their casks became coated with scum; then it turned yellow, and by the end of the year it stank so overpoweringly that the men had to hold their noses before they could drink it. The crew became listless; dark circles appeared under their eyes; their limbs started to ache and their gums to turn blue and swell. Six weeks out from the Strait of Magellan men began to die.

They died painfully and without dignity, their bodies emaciated, their breath foetid and their joints grotesquely swollen. They died of a disease they called simply 'the plague', but which we know today to have been scurvy.

Scurvy was the bane of sixteenth- and seventeenth-century seamen. They could neither prevent it nor cure it. They could only suffer it. And no one has depicted their suffering more poignantly than the Dutchman Roggeween (writing of his voyage across the Pacific when more than half his ship's company died):

No pen can describe the misery of life in our vessels. Only God knows how much we have suffered. Our vessels reeked of sickness and death. The stricken wailed and lamented day and night, and their

'Six weeks out from the Strait of Magellan men began to die'

cries would have moved stones to pity. Some became so emaciated that they looked like walking corpses and death blew them out like so many candles. Others became very fat and blown up like balloons; these were so afflicted with dysentery that they passed nothing but blood except for two or three days before they died when their excrement was like grey sulphur – and this was a sure sign that their hour had come. All were overcome by a fearful melancholy. . . . Even those who were not seriously ill, like myself, were left weak and enfeebled. My teeth were loose in my gums, which were swollen up almost to the thickness of a thumb, and my body was covered with swellings, red, yellow, green and blue in colour and the size of hazelnuts.

First to die was the younger of the Patagonian giants (whom Magellan, in spite of his initial setback, had managed to 'persuade' aboard). In their early days in the Pacific the crew had marvelled at the giant's strength, watching in amazement as he bent the steel shafts of their harquebuses and consumed at a single sitting a bushel of ship's biscuit and a three-litre pail of water. But his strength was no defence against the ravages of scurvy; his gums and his joints swelled up, his body broke out in sores and he became so weak that he could neither speak nor stand. His death is described by Pigafetta with unintended pathos: 'When the giant became sick, he asked for the Cross and frequently kissed and embraced it. Just before he died he told us that he wished to become a Christian. And we baptised him Paul.'

By mid-January over a third of Magellan's crew were so weak that they were unable to walk without the aid of a stick, and no more than a handful of men in each vessel were strong enough to work the sails or the helm. Water was rationed to a single scum-coated sip a day. The allowance of food was more generous: six ounces of ship's biscuit; but the biscuit was little more than powder, full of worm and weevil and stained yellow with the urine of rats. The rats themselves were a luxury, the mange-ridden corpses changing hands for half a year's pay.

On 20 January Magellan flung his charts into the sea: 'With the pardon of the cartographers,' he cried in despair, 'the Moluccas are not to be found at their appointed place.' And still the ships reeled on beneath skies which were unclouded by day, and filled by night with stars whose tranquil beauty was all the more poignant in contrast to the scene on which they looked down. For each vessel now was fast becoming a charnelhouse. Soon, although the crew must have known in theory that

FOLLOWING PAGES
A sixteenth-century artist's impression illustrating how the longitude of the earth can be found by the deviation of the magnet from the Pole. Peter Placius (1552–1622) is accredited with the discovery of this method.

155

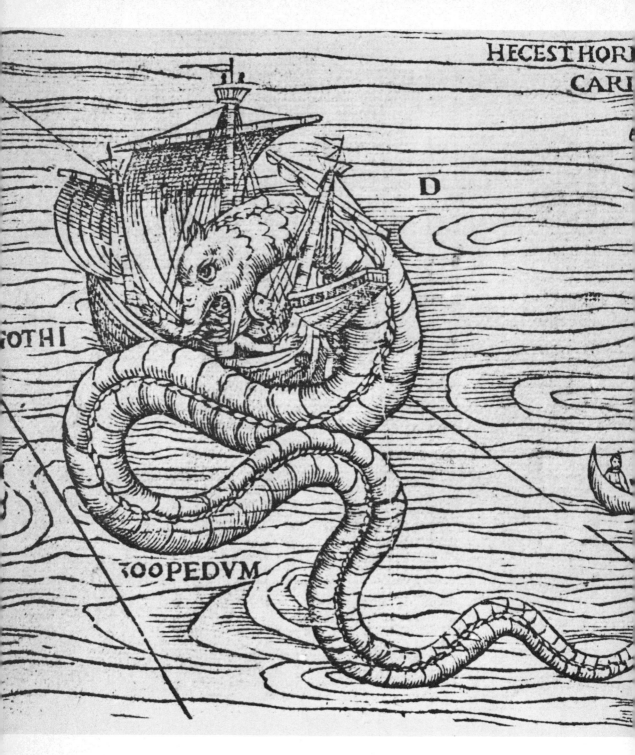

HECEST HOR[...]
CAR[...]

D

GOTHI

TOOPEDVM

A ship in the grip of a sea serpent,
from a Venetian map of 1539. Part of the
mythology of sixteenth-century seamen.

the world was round, they became obsessed with the age-old mariners' fear: that they had passed the world's last island, and were being blown down an unending waste of water which flowed on and on till it plunged in a mighty cataract clean off the surface of the earth.

But this fear at least proved groundless. For on the morning of St Paul's Day, 25 January, they sighted a low island, ringed by a lagoon and its periphery of surf. It was their first glimpse of land for almost exactly two months. The crew, by this time, were so debilitated by scurvy that no more than a handful of them, that first morning, had the strength to row the *bergantym* ashore.

Magellan named the island St Paul's; and although we cannot identify it with complete certainty it was probably Pukapuka, the most northerly of the Tuamotus. And here again Magellan was desperately unlucky. Had he been some fifteen or twenty miles to the south, he would have fallen in with a continuous succession of islands (the Tuamotus, the Society Islands, the Cook Islands, the New Hebrides and the Solomon Islands) which would have led him step by step to his goal. As it was, on leaving St Paul's his course of west-north-west took him away from the archipelagos of the South Pacific into one of the loneliest seaways on earth.

The armada spent the better part of a week on St Paul's. There was little water and no wood – the only vegetation being a dwarf magnolia which was all leaf and no stem – but in every other respect the island was a convalescents' paradise. In the deep water beyond the reef were bonita and albacore; in the shallow water of the lagoon were shoals of small, brightly-coloured fish. On the south-east side of the island – where wind and wave had pyramided the coral into a sculptor's fantasy of serac and pool – were crabs and *bêches de mer*; on the north-west side – where sandy beaches ran down to the lagoon – were clutches of turtles' eggs. And everywhere were sea birds and their eggs. This abundance of food soon brought about a return of strength and a rise in spirits. And on their third day on the island their other major problem, the shortage of water, was also resolved. The butts had just been brought ashore to be scoured, when the sky turned dark and a squall of rain bore down on the island. The men quickly spread out the sails of the *naos*, and in less than an hour several hundred litres of sweet fresh water had been caught and funnelled into the casks.

Had Magellan's fleet been only fifteen to twenty miles to the south of their course, it would have encountered a continuous succession of islands such as the Tuamotus, the Society Islands (pictured here), the Cook Islands, the New Hebrides and the Solomon Islands, which would have interspersed their arduous journey across the vast expanses of the Pacific with idyllic stopovers.

The fleet left St Paul's Island on 28 January. Though many of the crew were still weak and debilitated, they were in good spirits. For they were convinced they had now reached the skein of offshore islands which, they had been told, extended east from the coast of Asia; and they felt sure that from now on they would make frequent landfalls till they came to their goal.

The truth was not so roseate: far from having crossed the Pacific, they had traversed little more than a third of it.

To start with, hopes were high as the armada again stood west-north-west. But as the days lengthened into weeks and no more islands were sighted their anxiety returned. With the unrelenting wind from astern there could be no thought of turning back, and the *naos* had no choice but to reel on and on through a sea of glass, watched by a brazen sun by day and a haloed moon by night. They were athwart the Equator now; the sun was unrelenting, and their provisions were not of the sort to last. By mid-February the birds they had salted on St Paul's had been metamorphosed to a turmoil of worms, and the *bêches de mer* to hard little fragments of shell. Soon they were back to their single sip of water a day, and to hunting rats.

On 13 February they sighted more land (probably Vostok Island): a small, uninhabited atoll fringed with coconut palms. The crew staggered joyfully to the bow. But their joy was short-lived. For they were unable to land.

Nothing in all Magellan's circumnavigation of the world pinpoints more clearly than this incident the difficulties which sixteenth-century seamen had to face. Three vessels, with their crews literally dying of hunger, sighted an island in mid-ocean; the weather was fine; the sea was calm; and although the crews may have been weak they were certainly capable of manœuvring their ships. They ran up to the island, expecting to find shallow water close to its reef. But the water proved unexpectedly deep; too deep for them to anchor; the three vessels, one after the other, found themselves swept past the island, and once past it the wind was too strong for them to claw their way back. The three captains – Magellan, Serrano and del Cano – were all magnificent seamen. Yet to such a degree were their vessels at the mercy of wind and wave, that all they could do was to go on sounding, with hopeless persistence, long after all hope of plumbing bottom had gone. They were still sounding when the island sank slowly beneath the horizon and they were alone.

Their voyage became more and more terrible. On 4 March

'They were back to their single sip of water a day, and to hunting rats' the crew of the *Trinidad* ate the last of their food. At the bottom of their bread casks were one or two tiny fragments of overbaked biscuit, hard as flint and yellow with urine. These Magellan ordered to be pounded into a paste, which, when mixed with sawdust and water, he served to his dying ship's company as gruel. When this was gone there was quite literally nothing left in the flagship to eat: neither crumb nor bone, maggot nor shell. Magellan must have known that night that if he did not sight land within forty-eight hours every man in his armada would be dead.

8 Triumph and Disaster

THE DAY OF 5 MARCH dawned in much the same manner for Magellan as every other day had dawned in the last three months: a cloudless sky, a brassy sun, a blistering wind from astern. 'During all our time in the Pacific,' Pigafetta writes, 'we had no storm . . . and if our Lord had not aided us by giving us such good weather we would surely every one of us have perished in this great and terrible sea.' For some weeks now the *naos* had not lowered sail by night, partly because the crew were too weak and partly because Magellan was trying desperately to cover as great a distance as he could before the last of his food and water was used up. Sunrise on 5 March was therefore accompanied by none of the usual bustle and activity of squaring off the ship and adjusting her rig; there was nothing for the crew to do; they could only lie inert on the deck, awaiting an end which must by now have seemed inevitable. Aboard Magellan's *naos* nineteen men had already died, more than twenty were so weak they could hardly stand, and less than a dozen were capable of any sort of work. The day must have seemed endless.

A little before sunset one of the seamen was, as usual, ordered aloft to search for reefs. The seaman's name was Navarro, and he was the only man aboard with sufficient strength in his arms to climb the ratlines. Navarro spent longer than usual that evening scanning the horizon, and when he came down he mumbled that he had seen 'a cloud that looked like land'. For more than a fortnight now the crew had been sighting hallucinatory islands; nobody else could see Navarro's 'land', and several of the crew entered into a wager with him that he was wrong.

That night, for the first time in ninety-seven days, the wind dropped and the armada lost way. The atmosphere became airless and oppressive, and the three ships spun this way and that uneasily, drifting west like flotsam in the grip of an unseen current.

Next morning, as soon as the sky began to lighten, Navarro again struggled into the shrouds. He peered this way and that. And what he saw must have seemed for a moment too wonderful to be believed: fine on their starboard bow a great well-wooded island, its peaks rising reassuringly solid out of a veil of mist and cloud. Twice, we are told, Navarro's tongue ran round his lips. Twice his mouth opened but no sound came. Then a great cry was torn from his throat: 'Praise God! Land!

PREVIOUS PAGES A cloudless sky, a brassy sun and a blustering wind from astern greeted Magellan's fleet day after day during the latter part of their voyage across the Pacific. Weakened by scurvy and terrified by the apparently limitless extent of the new-found ocean, the men lay limply about the deck, awaiting an end they considered inevitable.

Land! Land!' and half-laughing, half-weeping in ecstasy, he came tumbling out of the shrouds.

For a moment none dared to believe him. Then man after man staggered to his feet and dragged himself to the rail to stare in rapture at the island which, as though by divine ordination, appeared at the moment they had quite lost hope. Some fell to their knees in prayer, some burst into tears, some indulged in strange gestures and grimaces, and those with sufficient strength hugged one another in ecstasy. Espinosa touched off the flagship's cannon; there were answering shots from the *Victoria* and the *Concepción*; Magellan unfurled the standard of Castile, and the priest led the ships' companies in the *Te Deum Laudamus*. No one begrudged Navarro the hundred-odd ducats he had won in bets!

Magellan's landfall was the Marianas, which he named Islas de las Velas Latinas (Islands of the Lateen Sails). The first island he sighted was probably Rota, and the one on which he eventually landed Guam. It took him, however, the better part of thirty hours to land, for much to his frustration a contrary current bore him past the first island and for some way parallel to the coast of a second. It was midday on 7 March before his vessels were able to nose into a small bay. Realising that his crew were probably too weak to lower sail, Magellan ordered the boatswain and a couple of seamen to stand by with axes; when he gave the signal the halyards were cut, the canvas descended with a rush and the *Trinidad* came to rest about a hundred yards offshore. The *Victoria* and the *Concepción* followed suit.

The men were trying, not very successfully, to launch the *bergantym*, when they found themselves surrounded by a veritable armada of canoes. These canoes were manned by natives with 'light tan skin, long brown hair, and the physique of gods'. For some moments they hovered about the *Trinidad*, circling and wheeling like a troupe of Bedouin horse, then they converged on her. One moment the waist of the flagship was empty; the next it was filled by upward of thirty stalwart natives, each armed with club, spear and oval shield – the latter decorated with tufts of human hair. The natives – who were members of a warrior elite, the Chamorros – took stock of the sickly Europeans and were obviously not impressed. Within seconds they had started a wholesale looting of anything they fancied; knives, ropes, canvas, axes, all were passed quickly

'Man after man staggered to his feet and dragged himself to the rail to stare in rapture'

Magellan's first landfall
following his crossing of the
Pacific was the Marianas. But
the indigenes, carrying shields
such as this, decorated with
tufts of human hair, boarded
his vessels on a rampage
of looting.

down to the waiting canoes. When one of the seamen tried to remonstrate, he was pushed aside so that he fell awkwardly to the deck. Magellan called his few able-bodied men to the poop.

What happened next may have been inevitable, but was none the less tragic.

The natives were asked to give back the items they had taken. They refused; and in the fracas which followed one of the seamen was flung contemptuously against the mast and another kicked into the scuppers. Magellan raised his hand. Six crossbows hummed. Six islanders fell writhing to the deck. For a moment their companions were quite unable to comprehend what had happened. Then they disappeared over the side. But they had the wit, even in retreat, to cut out and tow away the *bergantym*; and they dropped none of the items they had looted. Magellan cried out that the wounded were to be spared; but his crew, in their weakened condition, were taking no chances, and all but one of the natives were stabbed to death with halberd or sword.

Magellan has sometimes been condemned for this 'massacre of the innocents', but it is hard to see how he could have acted otherwise. There is, however, less justification for his next move, though one can appreciate the reasoning behind it – his overriding concern for the safety and health of his crew. The three *naos* stood close inshore and one after the other discharged a broadside into the Chamorros' village. The huts disintegrated. The natives fled. And Magellan led a landing party up the deserted beach. Their pillaging was swift, orderly and comprehensive. The butts were filled with water; everything edible (chickens, pigs, rice, bananas, coconuts and yams) was loaded into the recaptured *bergantym*; the outrigger canoes were destroyed to prevent pursuit; and as darkness fell the longboats, laden almost gunwale-under with food and drink, were rowed back in triumph to the fleet. Magellan weighed anchor, and the vessels stood out to sea.

There followed an orgy of feasting. All night the cauldrons bubbled with savoury stews of chicken and pork. For those unable to bite, yams, bananas and rice were crushed to a pulp; while for those who found it difficult to swallow, Magellan mixed breadfruit and coconut milk into a gruel. But the greatest joy of all must have been the water, cool, sweet and aromatic; the crew drank and drank again; and though it would be idle to pretend that the nourishment of a single meal restored them

'Six islanders fell writhing to the deck'

For Magellan the arrival of
his fleet in the Philippines
was his journey's end; he
wanted to savour and explore
his triumph. For his Spanish
captains, however, the rich
Spice Islands to the south
were the goal for which they
had sailed more than halfway
round the world.

170

C de Maunado
Is Way
we
ri

Babuyanes
C Baxador
water
I de Madato
I de Mirabra

C del Engano
Morio hermoso
R de Pintados

Il Siday
I Locos Costa
I Luzon braua
Sh Aquarina
A Paganfi
Panevasion
LUCO
Manilla
NI P de Mandato
A

P Escondido
P de Paiopos

PHILIPINÆ al.

G de Matalabombre
Pondam
Mandato
deMANILA. I.

Streto de Manila

Mindora

Dogeye
Panama

Il Catandanis
S Bernardo
Bay la Baya
Capull
C del Spirito Santo
Francisco Gomez
Primeiro Surgider

Tandaca

Ab camucho primiero
Cubarao

Pasagem de S
Clam

Suricao
Lomiaton
Dapito
MINDANAO
Forcador
Isytae
Mindanao

B de Malega

B de Resurreicam
B Bisaia
C Bicay

I de S.
Michael

I das Palme
iras

Tagema
Solor Candagary
I. la Matam
Sagim
Sninck

Carangaon

I da Doy

Boqueiram

Pangicaz
Bedroch
Manado
Ternate
Tidore
Pulo Cauallo
Timoralauor
Machian

Meaos

Cotta prinos

Cham
Camafa
I Noba
Patane
Papoos
I dos Graos

Magach area
la Tetolli

Bachian

Batochina

CELE
Cellebus
BES.

Mamoya
Burquj
Mandan
Puenga del vel Ba
Supa tochina
Malique

Zeram I.

Bilato
Xulla
Baorn

Budacuan
Cadapam
Vusasira
Mintam
tombu

Pacer

Tello

Xulla

Supino
Cambella

Caylon
Patines

Nuselaut

Gulguli

Muhisura
Ranata

Cambni

Belao
Amboina

Pulo Lappetseque
Banda

Goemeape

De Valaront
Streto de Celebes Boguroner
I Desolus
Anparuto
I Baly
I Gunoapie

Battaloya
Batatora
C de Flores
C terra alta

Pulurium Regis
Spuer Van Battang

Ferro
Lifaending
Terra Alta
Guliam

I Timor

150

to health, this was the turning-point on their road to recovery.

The night, however, was not given over entirely to feasting. For as the moon rose, the wind faded and died; the ships lost way; and soon the canoes of the Chamorros were putting out from every inlet along the coast. There were literally hundreds of them; they soon overtook the becalmed vessels and began to circle them, the rowers keening and mouthing abuse, and showering their decks with stones, filth and the occasional spear. Magellan ordered the carronades to be loaded with stones, but told his gunners not to fire unless the canoes made a concerted attack. It was as well for all concerned that soon after midnight the wind strengthened and the fleet made good its escape.

In spite of the unfortunate circumstances of his landfall, Magellan was now sailing in triumph. He had discovered and crossed the world's greatest ocean; he had, at the last moment, saved his ships' companies from what had looked like certain death; and now to crown his achievements he was told by the captured Chamorros that the Spice Islands were no more than a few days' sailing to the south. His captains and pilots urged him to alter course into sea-lanes that were familiar and known to be lucrative. Magellan, however, continued obstinately to the west. *His* goal was the Philippines.

For several days the fleet pursued a leisurely course, passing a number of small well-wooded islands, where they put in to replenish their supplies. Magellan was anxious firstly to get well clear of the Marianas, and secondly to find a haven where he could lie up while his crew convalesced; and on 16 March, the Feast of St Lazarus, he saw ahead a high continuous coastline, flanked by a skein of atolls. Although he did not realise it at the time, he had come at last to his journey's end. For the land he sighted was almost certainly Samar, the most easterly of the Philippines and the following is an account of their next few weeks:

We now found ourselves in shallow water, with a great multitude of islands at every point of the compass. These were fair as Eden, with gold beaches, graceful palms, exotic fruits and soil so rich that if one snapped off a twig and stuck it into the ground it would start straightway to grow. One island [probably Homonhon] was set apart a little from the rest; it had a good anchorage and appeared to be uninhabited; and here Magellan decided we would put ashore to recuperate. The next few weeks were like some summer idyll. We built a stockade on one of the bluffs overlooking the harbour, and here in the shade of

'He had come
at last to
his journey's end'

a cluster of breadfruit trees we set up shelters to accommodate the sick. As soon as a camp was established the more able-bodied were given leave to hunt, fish and explore the island. We found it a hunters' paradise, especially rich in fruit – mango, mangosteen and papaya: taro, breadfruit and custard-apple: oranges, yams and the ubiquitous coconut. It was these fruits, I believe, which were the main cause of our recovery. These and the tenderness of Magellan. For with the halt and the lame the Captain-General proved himself gentle as a woman. Each morning he would visit those still confined to their bed; with his own hands he would help to prepare a gruel from the roots of the taro plant. 'Get well soon,' he would say to them. 'For nothing awaits you now but cloves and gold and the women of the islands.' And the men trusted him, knowing that no other captain could have led us through so many and so diverse perils to within sight of our goal.[1]

A passage which emphasises one of Magellan's more attractive traits: though he drove his crew hard, he cared for them with a compassion reminiscent of that other *primus inter pares* of explorers, Cook.

They spent the better part of a fortnight on Homonhon, sailing at dawn on 27 March. And the day after they left the island there took place one of the most dramatic incidents of the voyage.

In the early morning of 28 March 1521, they sighted a large canoe manned by eight natives. Black Henry hailed them in Malay, and in Malay – for the first time in all their voyage – he was answered. The natives were shy; but eventually they were persuaded to exchange gifts with the crew of the *Trinidad*; and among the presents they brought aboard were porcelain jars decorated with a design which was unmistakably Chinese.

The sea that morning was placid and the sky serene; the canoe looked much like any other canoe, and the natives like any other men. Yet as Magellan fingered the Chinese jars and listened to Black Henry conversing in Malay, it must have come to him quite suddenly that this was the goal for which he had suffered so much and for so long: that after 550 days of storm and mutiny, hunger, pestilence and death, he had circumnavigated the world.

Events now moved swiftly to a climax: a climax which may appear at first sight to be unexpected, but which one can see in retrospect has all the predetermined pathos of Greek tragedy.

[1] From James Vance Marshall's novel based on Magellan's voyage: *The Wind at Morning*, to be published in 1973 by Hart-Davis, MacGibbon.

This was the known world
when Magellan set sail, as
depicted *c.* 1520 by Jean
Schoener – a professor of
mathematics at Nuremberg.
Magellan's circumnavigation
was to show what lay on the
other side of the globe.

SEPTENTRIO

MERIDIES

ORIENS

From this moment the scene of Magellan's activities shifts from sea to land – an environment in which he was never so happy. Also the challenge facing him shifts from a challenge of the elements to a challenge of people. Over the past eighteen months Magellan had proved himself a brilliant practical explorer, well able to cope with the vagrancies of wind, wave and solitude, but his armada was now about to enter one of the most highly populated, civilised and sophisticated areas on earth, and the qualities needed from its commander were no longer resource and seamanship but patience and diplomacy – neither of which had ever been Magellan's forte. Another problem also now came to the fore. During much of the voyage the fact that Magellan's goal was the Philippines and his men's goal the Moluccas had not greatly mattered, for the two places were close enough for the same course to serve for either. Now, however, at their journey's end they had fetched up in the Philippines. Magellan was content. His men, on the other hand, regarded these islands as no more than a stepping stone on their way to the Spiceries; no sooner had they arrived than they were fretting to be away.

These problems were obscured for the time being by the warmth of Magellan's welcome in the Philippines, and by the discovery of gold.

In the afternoon of 28 March the Rajah or potentate of the island by which they were anchored came aboard. He was shown over the flagship, invited to witness a simulated fight to demonstrate the effectiveness of armour and laden with valuable gifts. He and Magellan got on so well in fact that they performed the Malay ritual of *Cassi Cassi*, tasting one another's blood and swearing everlasting friendship – an oath which both, incidentally, were scrupulously to honour. That night a number of the crew were entertained in the Rajah's palace. Next day the vessels dropped anchor close inshore, and there followed an orgy of feasting, fornicating and trading which surpassed even the Saturnalia in Rio. For to the men's lust for women was now added the sharper and more acquisitive lust for gold, which was now found in abundance. We know from Pigafetta that the Rajah himself had gold accoutrements:

'There followed an orgy of feasting, fornicating and trading'

He was a most handsome person with black hair down to his shoulders, and two large gold rings dangling from his ears. At his side he wore a dagger with a long handle wrought entirely in gold . . . many of his household vessels were likewise of this metal.

It seems, however, to have been the Rajah's brother, a dignitary from the nearby island of Mindanao, who triggered off what developed into a mini gold rush. Parr tells us:

This man not only wore many gold ornaments and had gold-mounted weapons, but he had three little spots of gold, spaced in a triangle, mounted in each of his front teeth, so that when he smiled his whole mouth glittered. He told the Spaniards that all his household utensils were of gold, and sent a canoe back to his home to bring some of the metal which could be used in trade. The canoe returned with a sack that was filled with nuggets the size of a hen's egg; and these he proceeded to exchange on an even basis, pound for pound, for iron.

Magellan cautioned his men not to show too much eagerness, lest they spoil the market. But in a couple of days his vessels were virtually stripped of iron, and each of his crew had amassed, by personal bargaining, a small fortune.

Magellan's personal disinterest in gold was offset by his obsession for more spiritual matters: and he developed a sudden addiction to proselytising. As Parr puts it:

The people were friendly, and the Spaniards mingled with them without fear of treachery. On Easter Sunday a solemn High Mass was celebrated ashore, with a salute of six guns at the moment of the Elevation of the Host. The natives, who were pagans not Mohammedans, were delighted with this ceremony; and much to Magellan's satisfaction, many expressed a desire to become Christians. He erected a large cross on a hill overlooking the palace, and formally took possession for Spain of the entire archipelago, which he named the Islands of St Lazarus.

'Many natives expressed a desire to become Christians'

And if one is tempted to smile at this and other still more grandiose ceremonies to come, it is worth remembering that Spanish culture and the Catholic faith have endured for four and a half centuries in the Philippines, which are today the only predominantly Christian nation in Asia.

On 2 April Magellan called the conference which was to mark the watershed of his fortunes. His officers begged him yet again to head for the Moluccas; even John Serrano, who had hitherto followed him without question, added his voice to that of the Spanish captains – for the very good reason that he knew his brother Francisco was awaiting him in Ternate with a valuable cargo. Magellan, however, insisted that the fleet push still deeper into the Philippines.

FOLLOWING PAGES This map of the world shows the route taken by Magellan and his expedition. Notice the incomplete outlines of the Americas which had been discovered thirty years before Magellan's voyage, and the absence of Australia and New Zealand, which (like most of the islands of the Pacific) were still unknown to Europeans.

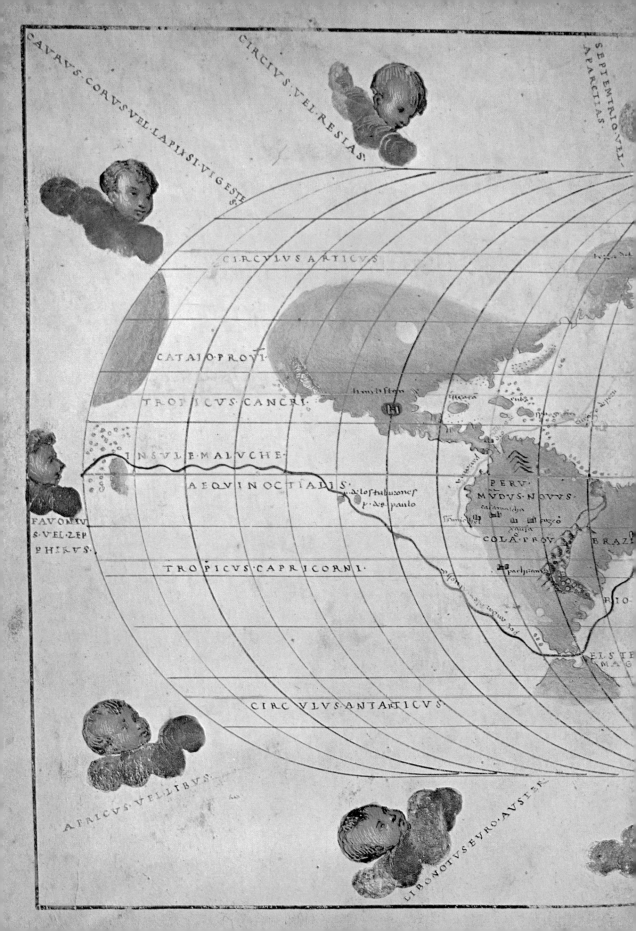

Three factors, I think, influenced his decision. Firstly, he must have felt that having sailed some twenty thousand miles and discovered what was virtually an unknown archipelago, it would be unenterprising not to explore this great new discovery, especially since several of the islands appeared to be rich in gold. Secondly, he must have been anxious to reach a landmark which he recognised from his voyage of 1510-11; for only when he did this would he be certain, beyond all possible doubt, that he had actually circumnavigated the world. Thirdly, he had personal reasons for wanting to discover more than six new islands, since his royal charter expressly laid down that 'should you discover more than six new lands, you shall have particular rights to any two of them . . . on you, and on your sons and heirs in perpetuity, shall be confirmed the title of *adelantado* [governor] of such lands'.

These were weighty reasons. Nevertheless, Magellan would have been well advised to attach even more weight to the advice of his officers – if only because in the kaleidoscope of diplomacy, negotiating, trading and proselytising which lay ahead, he was to need their support far more than he had ever needed it in the open reaches of the sea. He made no concessions, however, to their wishes. And it was with mixed feelings that on 3 April the armada once again turned its back on the Spice Islands and stood north-west into the heart of the Philippines.

To start with, there was no indication of the disaster to come. Magellan's blood-brother, the Rajah Colombu, provided an armada of canoes to escort the *naos* to the nearby island of Cebu, and for three days the vessels picked their way through a skein of atolls each, it seemed, richer and more beautiful than the one before. Twice a landing party was sent ashore for water, and on each occasion the men brought back glowing reports of the fertile soil, the exotic *flora* and *fauna* and the thick gold ornaments worn by the women. On 6 April they sighted Cebu and ran for some time parallel to its coast, much impressed by the prosperous fishing villages, each with its traps and weir staked out for several hundred yards into the sea. As they progressed up the coast more and more canoes, many with brightly-coloured sails, attached themselves to the fleet, so that by nightfall they had an escort of almost a thousand vessels. Their voyage had been transformed into a ceremonial procession.

On the morning of 7 April they entered the principal port of Cebu, and Magellan was rowed ashore to pay his repects to

'Their voyage had been transformed into a ceremonial procession'

the Rajah. Up to now he had been dealing with simple, relatively unimportant people; but the Rajah of Cebu seems to have been a potentate of considerable power, suavity and sophistication; he had with him both Chinese and Arab advisers – and the latter at any rate can hardly have been overjoyed at the arrival of a Christian fleet.

It is not too easy to interpret the events of the next few weeks. The Rajah was an enigmatic character, much given to long silences and the chewing of betel nut. It is probable that he had heard of the devastation the white men had brought in their wake at Dabul, Goa and Malacca, and he must have been anxious not to provoke them; on the other hand he probably wished with all his heart that they had never arrived. After a good deal of sabre-rattling and diplomatic manœuvring to prevent either party losing face, Magellan's *naos* were given permission to anchor and to trade without paying the customary dues. There followed an almost incredible fortnight of debauchery, barter and religious mania.

The crew had had no women since leaving Brazil. The girls of Cebu worked the paddy-fields naked as Eve. As Parr sententiously remarks, 'when the men were given shore leave in this sensuous environment their reactions were inevitable. . . . As in Rio, a lad who had a knife or a few fish-hooks could obtain all the feminine companionship he wished.' A few of the men may have overstepped the mark – Carvalho, for instance, seems to have led a raid on the Rajah's harem – but by and large it is hard to see that their amorous activities did any harm.

Barter was equally frenetic. A warehouse and exchange market was set up ashore. Magellan unloaded his copper, quicksilver, bracelets, mirrors, scissors and knives, together with all the iron he could lay his hands on. The Filipinos brought their chickens, ginger, rice, sugarcane, silk, inlaid boxes, pearls and precious and semi-precious stones; and their gold. An equable basis for exchange was quickly agreed, the most significant rate being '10 pieces of gold for 14 lb of iron'; and Pigafetta tells us that both Europeans and Filipinos scrupulously observed the prescribed rates. It therefore seems as though trade, like sex, pleased all and harmed none. What *was* responsible then for the welter of treachery and bloodshed which erupted with such terrible violence at the end of the month?

An easy answer would be Christianity: the sort of forcible attempts at conversion which were the cause of so much misery

A fleet of canoes such as
these met Magellan in
the Philippines – they bore
gifts and led the ships through
the cluster of islands.

in South America. This, however, would be unfair to Magellan. It was certainly his religious zeal which sparked off the tragedy, but the tinder on which the flames fed was the antipathy of his Spanish officers and their failure to stand by him at the time he needed them most.

The first act of the tragedy is described by Stefan Zweig:

Before long relations between Filipinos and Europeans grew so cordial that the Rajah and many of his followers expressed a desire to become Christians. Let Pigafetta tell us how Magellan replied to this request: 'The Captain-General warned them against adopting Christianity either from fear or in the hope of pleasing him. If they really wished to become Christians, he said, they must do so for the love of God; and if they did not become Christians, the Spaniards would do them no harm. They then declared, as with one voice, that they wished to become Christians of their own free will. The Captain-General then embraced them with tears in his eyes, and swore that from henceforth they should live in perpetual peace with the King of Spain.'

Next Sunday, 14th April, the Spaniards celebrated their greatest triumph. In the centre of the town a great dais was erected and hung with decorations and palm fronds. Carpets were brought from the ship, together with two thrones swathed in velvet. In front of these was placed the altar. These preparations were watched by literally thousands of natives. The Captain-General now made a dramatic entry; banners were unfurled, a salute was fired from the ships, and the Rajah and his family, kneeling in front of the Cross, were duly baptised. . . . The news spread far and wide. And next day there came from the neighbouring islands many more dignitaries to be initiated in these magical ceremonies. Within a few days almost all the chiefs of the Philippines had pledged their troth to Spain and been sprinkled with the waters of baptism. . . . Seldom has a great deed been more splendidly accomplished. Magellan had discovered the strait leading to the other side of the world; new islands with abundant riches had been won for the Crown of Castile; countless souls had accepted the true faith – and, triumph above triumphs, these things had been done without shedding a drop of blood. . . . What other conquistadors achieved only after many years – and then with the aid of the rack, the Inquisition and burnings at the stake – Magellan had achieved in a few days and wholly without violence.

Magellan's success, however, seems to have gone to his head. Baptisms, processions, services and pious proclamations now followed one another in a flood – indeed on the armada's third Sunday in Cebu there were so many baptisms that by the end of the day the priests lacked sufficient strength to raise their

'Banners were unfurled, a salute was fired, and the Rajah and his family, kneeling in front of the Cross, were duly baptised'

arms in blessing. This, of course, was entirely laudable. But neither the bulk of Magellan's men, nor the bulk of his officers, were in the least impressed. The men coveted the Filipinos' bodies not their souls, and the officers, having exhausted the immediate market in gold, were anxious to head south for the Spice Islands. It was at this critical moment that Magellan committed the blunder which cost him his life.

The Rajah of Cebu told him that a number of chiefs in the outlying islands had failed to abandon the gods of their ancestors and were continuing to worship their idols. Whether the Rajah had ulterior motives in disclosing this is hard to say. Magellan, at any rate, reacted in exactly the manner the Rajah may, perhaps, have hoped. 'The chiefs', he said, 'shall be punished.'

His council implored him not to become involved in local politics – such a course of action, apart from anything else, was expressly forbidden by the *Casa de Antillas*. Magellan, however, was determined to make an example of the recalcitrant chiefs, and he sent Espinosa and his marines to bring the most powerful of them, Cilapulapu, to heel. This was done in the time-honoured manner. Cilapulapu's defences were stormed, his warriors were massacred, his women were ravished, and his capital razed by fire. And if today this seems a terrible thing to have done, it can only be said in part-mitigation that in the sixteenth century it was no more than common practice.

Magellan must have hoped that Cilapulapu would now be cowed. The chieftain, however, proved a man of spirit, for although he agreed reluctantly to pay homage he refused to pay tribute. Egged on by the Rajah of Cebu, Magellan decided to break him, probably trying to justify this decision by telling himself that once Cilapulapu had been subjugated, the whole archipelago would be swiftly converted to Christianity.

Some writers have expressed the view that there is only one explanation of the events of the next forty-eight hours: 'Magellan was suffering from religious hysteria.' A simpler explanation is that for the past twenty months Magellan had played a lone hand. Time and time again he had gone against the advice of his council and been proved right; so it is hardly to be wondered at that he now preferred his judgment to theirs. The tragedy was that his judgment on land was nothing like so sound as at sea, and he had, during the last few weeks, lost his sense of direction and become like a man with a death-wish,

INSVLA MATHAN

Victoria

Magellan's religious zeal led to his becoming embroiled in a battle with a tribal chief on the island of Mactan; this woodcut depicts his landing party advancing on the natives.

driven by forces beyond his control toward an end which all but he could see was inevitable. The simple seamen who loved him lacked the perspicacity to stop him; the Spanish officers who hated him hardly bothered to try.

On the evening of Friday, 26 April, Magellan informed his council that he was determined to punish Cilapulapu. They remonstrated in vain. He told them he had decided to lead the punitive party in person. Again they remonstrated in vain. 'And I shall take with me', he added, 'none but volunteers. We shall see then whose trust is in God.' The Spanish officers, who by this time were heartily sick of Magellan and his proselytising, failed to volunteer; so did Espinosa and his marines, who were piqued that they had not been chosen to lead the landing party as a matter of course. Magellan's blood-brother offered to re-inforce him with a thousand well-trained warriors; but the Captain-General told him that the soldiers of Christ had no need of earthly aid, and that God would lead them to victory.

The landing party assembled at midnight: a motley contingent of common seamen, stewards, serving men and pages, no more than sixty in number. Magellan was the only officer among them with the slightest experience of leading a foray ashore. If he had any qualms about the size and composition of his force, he hid them. He simply distributed armour and weapons, and in the small hours of the morning the expedition embarked in its longboats.

Everything went wrong. Instead of launching a surprise attack, Magellan first sent an envoy to Cilapulapu, demanding his fealty. When this was refused, he attempted to land, but found that the tide was not yet high enough for his boats to clear the coral reefs which guarded the shore. For several hours the landing party were obliged to lay-to, the men shivering in the sea mist and plagued by mosquitoes; and at the end of it all, much to their chagrin, they were ordered to wade the 200 yards to the shore. They landed at sunrise, cold, wet and in none-too-good a temper, to find the better part of 3,000 [natives] drawn up in the form of a crescent to oppose them.[1]

Sixty men against three thousand may sound long odds; it should, however, be remembered that Pizarro conquered Peru with nineteen men, and that the Spaniards' armour and crossbows gave them an incalculable advantage. At any rate, Magellan advanced confidently enough till he came to a series

[1] From James Vance Marshall's novel based on Magellan's voyage: *The Wind at Morning*, to be published in 1973 by Hart-Davis, MacGibbon.

of ditches which Cilapulapu had excavated, ostensibly to protect the village which lay in the centre of his lines. It was now that the landing party's lack of discipline and skill became painfully apparent; for though the crossbowmen made a fearsome noise their bolts did little damage, and they went on discharging long after Magellan had ordered 'cease fire', so that they nearly shot some of their own men who had started to scramble into the ditches. Eventually, however, the excavations were crossed without loss, the natives falling back with no more than token resistance. They were, Magellan realised, trying to draw him away from the boats; and to stop them retreating farther he ordered two of his young aides, Rabelo and de la Torre, to set fire to the village. The youngsters, however, never reached their objective; they were cut off by a sudden attack from the Filipinos. Magellan's covering fire was neither accurate enough nor heavy enough to save them, and they were overwhelmed by sheer weight of numbers and stabbed to death.

The shock seems to have brought Magellan to his senses. Realising for the first time the danger of his predicament, he gave the order to retire.

When the Filipinos saw the white men – whom up to now they had regarded as invincible – begin to retreat, they set up a jubilant fanfare on their conch-shells and launched an all-out attack. Magellan, however, conducted the first part of his withdrawal with no little skill, half his men providing covering fire while the other half crossed the ditches. Indeed they were three-quarters of the way to the safety of their boats when their inexperience proved fatal. Seeing the water's edge no more than a hundred yards ahead, and thinking they were in danger of being outflanked by the advancing Filipinos, they broke formation and began to rush, each man for himself, for the shore. Magellan and less than a dozen companions were left to cover their flight.

The events of the next hour make tragic reading.

When the panic-stricken Spaniards reached the water's edge they tumbled into the longboats, capsizing one and fighting for a place in the others. Then they pushed off and began to row post haste for the *naos*, leaving Magellan and his companions to their fate.

Incredible as it sounds, we are told by Pigafetta that the Captain-General and his handful of men managed to defend themselves for the better part of an hour against every assault

Isles des Larrons

Le capitaine arriue à ʒamal vindrent neuf hômmes
y aueccq des presens. Lhonneur quil leur fist. Des fruictz Coch
n de palme. Cordes a nattires. Pouldre a manger / facon de pain
u clere et cordiale. Huille / Vinaigre. Et laict faitz et concies
a fruictz venant des palmiers ⸺⸺⸺

Chapitre ⸺ xvi.ᵉ

Abmedi seziesme de mars. Mil cinq centz vingt et
vng nous arriuaimes au poinct du iour a vne
haulte isle loing de la susdicte isle des larrons
oys centz lieues. La quelle isle sappelle ʒʒamal. Et le iour
pres le capitaine general voulut descendre a vne aultre isle
sabitee pres de laultre pour estre plus en seurete et pour y
endre de leau. aussi pour se reposer la quelques iours. Ou il
st faire deux tentes en terre pour les malades et leur fist
er vne truye ⸺⸺⸺

Le capitaine arriue
a ʒʒamal descendit
a vne aultre isle.

E lundi dixhuytiesme de mars apres disner veismes
venir vers nous vne barque et neuf hommes dedans
ir quoy le capitaine general commanda que personne ne se
uliast ny parlast aulcunement sans son conge. Quand
s gentz furent venus en cette isle vers nous incontinent le plus
pparant dentreulx alla vers le capitaine general demonstrant
tre fort ioyeux de nostre venue. Et demourerent cinq des plus
pparans auecques nous / les aultres qui resterent a la barque al
rent leuer aulcuns qui peschoyent et apres vindrent tous ensem
le. Dont le capitaine voyant que ces gentz estoyent de raison /
ur fist bailler a boire et a manger et leur donna des bonnetz rou
s des miroers peignes sonnettes boucassins et aultres choses

Le Capitaine
venir des gens …
luy

De ceulx qui vindrent
vers le capitaine / Et
le traictement quil leur
fist /:

the three thousand natives launched on them. Even more incredible is the fact that the men who had been left behind in the *naos* made not the slightest effort to come to their aid. One by one Magellan's companions were bludgeoned to death, until only five, all desperately wounded, were left standing: the Captain-General himself, Black Henry, Pigafetta, de Escovar and the young marine Filiberto. And still the crew of the *naos*, which were anchored within hailing distance of the shore, stood passively by.

Only Magellan's blood-brother, the Rajah Colombu, rowed in tears from ship to ship beseeching each captain in turn to launch a rescue. But he found the Spanish officers smiling. 'This is Magellan's quarrel', he was told. 'It is not for us to interfere.' Beside himself with anxiety, Colombu ordered two of his largest canoes to row inshore to try to pick the survivors up. But there now took place an incident which shows very clearly the way those in command of the *naos* were thinking. Aboard the *Concepción* John Lopes Carvalho at last ordered his carronades to be loaded and fired. What he aimed at, however, was not the attacking Filipinos but the Rajah's canoes. Ten of Colombu's men were killed; his vessels were sunk; and with them disappeared the one chance of a last-minute rescue.

It was shortly after this that Magellan was slashed across the left leg by a scimitar. He collapsed face down in the sea. His companions did what they could to cover him with their shields; but sheer weight of numbers drove them into deep water. As they fell back, a group of warriors rushed at Magellan. And before he could rise, they struck him again and again with their spears in the face and legs. 'And so', laments Pigafetta, 'they slew our mirror, our light, our comfort and our true and only guide.'

As if this had been the signal for which they were waiting, as soon as Magellan fell the longboats moved inshore to pick up the survivors. The body of their Captain-General they made no effort to recover.

Magellan's epitaph is in Pigafetta's diary:
'. . . So noble a captain . . . he was more constant
than anyone else in adversity. He endured hunger
better than all the others, and better than any man
in the world did he understand sea charts and
navigation . . . the best proof of his genius is that he
circumnavigated the world, none having
preceded him.'

FERDINA MAGELLAN

1 5   2 0.

Patagones: Magelanici Fretum

Terra de fugo.

1 5   7 7.

FRANCI SCVS DRACO

Prima ego veliuolis ambiui
Magellane nouo   te duce
Ambiui. meritoq̃   vocor
Vela, alæ, preciũ,   gloria

VICTORIA.

Conueniunt rebus nomina ſe

9 The Survivors

PERHAPS THE MOST ELOQUENT TESTIMONY to Magellan's greatness is the chaos which followed his death. For he alone possessed the knowledge and force of character that was needed to hold the armada together; and with his hand no longer on the helm, his once-proud fleet drifted from disaster to disaster.

First, the officers walked into a trap and got themselves massacred.

They elected as their new commander Duarte Barbosa, who should have had the wit to realise that only two courses were open to him: either to cut his losses and run, or to carry out reprisals which would restore the Europeans' prestige. He did neither. Instead, he tried to negotiate simultaneously with Colombu, Cilapulapu and the Rajah of Cebu; and he was foolish enough to use as his mediator Black Henry, although a child might have realised that the slave was no friend of the men who had left his master to die.

Inevitably Black Henry and the Rajahs joined forces to dig a pit for the incompetent grandees to tumble into. They invited the dignitaries ashore, ostensibly to a dinner at which Barbosa was to be presented with a set of bejewelled regalia he was known to covet. With Magellan's blood scarcely dry on the Filipinos' spears, it seems incredible that the invitation should have been considered let alone accepted. But such was the Spaniards' stupidity and greed, that on the evening of 1 May thirty of the senior members of the fleet rowed blithely ashore. Included in their party were not only their commander-in-chief but all the captains, masters and pilots, most of the *alguacils* and *contramaestres*, and the fleet astrologer and priest. Within a couple of hours of landing, most of them were either drunk or paying court to the girls of the harem.

Only the sharp-eyed Espinosa and the long-eared Carvalho seem to have been in the least suspicious. In the middle of the banquet these two invented an excuse to leave, and managed to return undetected to the *naos*. They had scarcely hoist themselves aboard, when bedlam broke loose in the palace. At a pre-arranged signal the Spaniards were attacked, and though in the confusion that followed the building was set on fire and a handful of men managed briefly to defend themselves, in the end all but two were either stabbed or burned to death. The survivors were John Serrano and the priest. The priest seems to have been spared because, a few days earlier, he had won the

PREVIOUS PAGES The *Victoria*, the only survivor of the five vessels which sailed under Magellan. Of the 277 men who had left Spain in 1519, only eighteen returned, but the information they brought back was of incalculable value.

gratitude of the Rajah Colombu by curing his son of 'the colic'. Serrano saved himself – temporarily – by persuading his captors that he would fetch a goodly sum in ransom.

There now occurred an incident which shows very clearly the sort of men who had taken over the fleet. Here is Pigafetta's description of the aftermath of the massacre:

The *naos* hoist anchor, and, approaching the shore, discharged a broadside into the houses of the natives. When the smoke cleared, we saw that John Serrano, bound and wounded, had been dragged to the water's edge. He cried out that we should cease fire, or else the natives would kill him. We asked him if the others had all been massacred, and he replied 'Yes, except the priest.' He then begged us most earnestly to redeem his life with some merchandise – 'two lombards and a few copper bars'. But Carvalho, his one-time friend, was loth to do this, realising that if Serrano returned aboard he [Carvalho] would no longer be master of the fleet . . . .

Another broadside was poured into the village; then the ships, catching the night wind, began to draw quickly away from the shore.

Whereat John Serrano, weeping, shouted that once we sailed he would be killed. He would, he cried, pray to God that at the day of judgment he should ask Carvalho how and why he had been left to die. But our fleet departed with all the speed it could muster, and John Serrano was never heard of again.

Magellan's ships' company had come to Cebu as gods. They left, pursued by the abuse of the Filipinos, as thieves and murderers. And as thieves and murderers they lived for the next four months. For Carvalho turned to piracy.

His first move was to scuttle the *Concepción*. This may have been necessary; for of the 277 men who had sailed from Seville only 115 were still alive, and there were probably insufficient seamen to work three ships. What certainly *was not* necessary was that before Carvalho set fire to the *Concepción*, he transferred to her every one of Magellan's papers – his diary, logs, charts, invoices, even his personal letters. Carvalho's objective, of course, was to destroy incriminating evidence: to prevent Magellan – as it were from the grave – arraigning the men who by their mutiny, treachery and incompetence had transformed his voyage from a many-splendoured epic to an unhappy chronicle of man's inhumanity to man. In this he succeeded.

'They had come to Cebu as gods. They left as thieves and murderers'

For it is largely because of the lack of contemporary records that Magellan is not as well known today as he deserves to be. Indeed it would be no exaggeration to say that it was not only the *Concepción* which was fed that May afternoon to the flames: it was Magellan's rightful place in history.

Next day the *Trinidad* and the *Victoria* sighted a junk on her way from the Moluccas to China, and although the junk was on lawful trade they gave chase and boarded her; her crew were massacred, and her cargo of pepper and cloves transferred to the *naos*. It was the start of four months of thieving, murder and debauchery. For the shipping of the south-west Pacific was

Following the death of Magellan, his ships' companies embarked on four months' of piracy, murder and debauchery. On sighting a junk such as this, they gave chase, boarded, massacred her crew, and absconded with the cargo of pepper and cloves.

virtually unarmed and its ports no more than lightly defended; the carronades of the Spaniards were an argument which brooked no answer, and Carvalho was able to plunder more or less at will. In addition to his other exploits he kept aboard a harem of Muslim women. This inevitably led to quarrelling and bloodshed. And on 1 October Carvalho was deposed by a triumvirate, of whom the leading figure was Espinosa.

The *alguacil* was of humble birth and no navigator; but he had plenty of sound common-sense and was a leader of men. He restored discipline, set the women ashore and began to make his way from island to island, inquiring each time he

The unarmed trading ships of the south-west Pacific, pictured below, were easy prey to the guns of the *Victoria* and *Trinidad*.

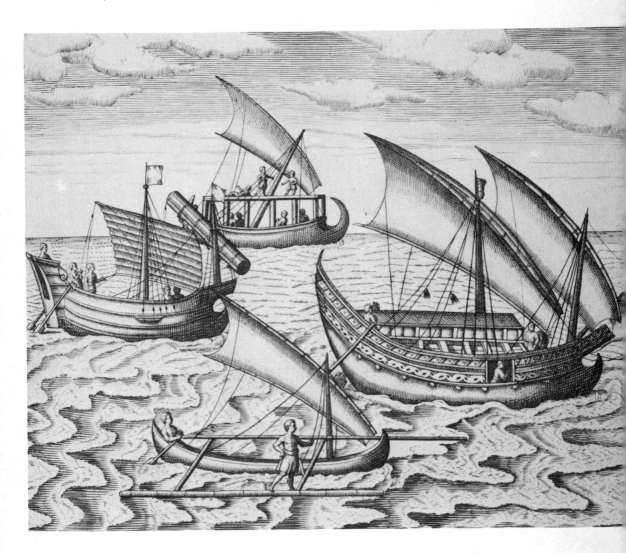

SVMATRA.

IAVA
MAIOR

Celebes.

Draco

INSVLA TERNATE.

Under the more sagacious leadership of Espinosa, the *Trinidad* and the *Victoria* came at last to the Spice Islands. Here, as depicted in this woodcut, they were welcomed and showered with gifts.

landed, 'In which direction are the Moluccas?' And at last, in November 1521, the twin peaks of Tidor and Ternate were sighted, rising out of the quiet sea. After a voyage of 820 days and 28,000 miles the *Trinidad* and the *Victoria* had come at last to their goal.

Magellan's cousin, Francisco Serrano, had described the Spice Islands as 'a New World, richer, greater and more beautiful than that of Vasco da Gama'; and his judgment was now confirmed by Espinosa and his men. For the King of Tidor welcomed them as friends of long standing, acknowledging fealty to Spain, allowing them ashore to live and to trade and showering them with a great quantity of valuable presents without expecting so much as a bale of cloth in return. It must have seemed to the exhausted seamen that they had come to the Islands of the Blessed.

They spent three months in Tidor, resting, recuperating, trading and helping to build a fort which would command the entrance to the harbour. And in all this time there is no record of bloodshed, disagreement or indeed of so much as an angry word. Early in 1522, however, Espinosa's thoughts turned to their passage home. Bilges were scoured, sails were patched, waterbutts were filled and their cargo – the fruits of two years' trade and four months' piracy – was invoiced and loaded into the holds. And what a cargo it was! Pigafetta quotes some dozen lines from the manifest:

> Many bahars of cloves, plumage of the birds of the terrestrial paradise, roots of ginger dried in jars, white parrots called catara and red speaking parrots known as nori, honey from bees which were small as ants, very many quintals of pepper both round and long, nutmeg, cinnamon, sandalwood, small quantities of fine white gold ... robes of silk, porcelain, patoles [lengths of gold and silk from China], and a great quantity of golden ornaments and precious jewels.

Indeed so much was packed into the *naos'* holds that the *Trinidad* quite literally burst her seams and foundered in the mud of the estuary – an undignified end for the vessel which had so proudly led her consorts across three quarters of the world.

It was the second week of February when the flagship foundered, and Espinosa, afraid of missing the monsoon, decided that half his men should sail at once in the *Victoria* while the other half remained to try to recaulk and refloat the *Trinidad*. They drew lots to decide who should go and who

'The King of Tidor welcomed them as friends of long standing, acknowledgeing fealty to Spain'

After three months' trading in the Spice Islands, the ships' holds were bulging with 'cloves, plumage of the birds of paradise, honey, white and red parrots, dried ginger, quintals of pepper, nutmeg, cinnamon, sandalwood, silk, porcelain, golden ornaments, precious jewels and small quantities of fine white gold'. These drawings show some of the cargo. OPPOSITE is a nutmeg just before it drops its fruit; BELOW: the leaf, trunk and bark of the cinnamon tree, and BELOW RIGHT: the root and stalk of the ginger plant.

should stay, and on 13 February 1522 forty-seven Europeans and thirteen 'Indians' under the command of the Basque del Cano stood west in the *Victoria*. After two and a half years they were homeward bound.

It would be pleasant to record that Espinosa, who had contributed more than anyone alive to the circumnavigation, refloated the *Trinidad* and returned in triumph to Spain. The truth is not so roseate. He and his crew were captured by the Portuguese and hanged as pirates. Thus the evil wrought by Carvalho lived after him, while the courage and loyalty of the *alguacil* has failed to win the recognition it deserves.

Del Cano had not up to now played a particularly distinguished role in the circumnavigation – indeed at St Julian he had been one of the mutineers – but the hour made the man. His task was a formidable one: to sail an old, storm-battered and overladen vessel for more than ten thousand miles without putting into land – for the ports between Tidor and Europe

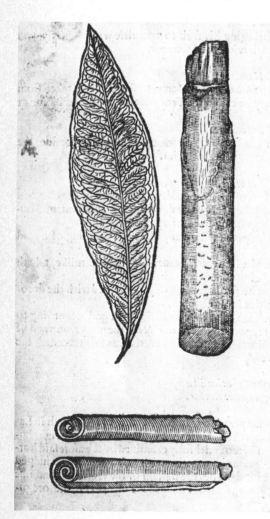

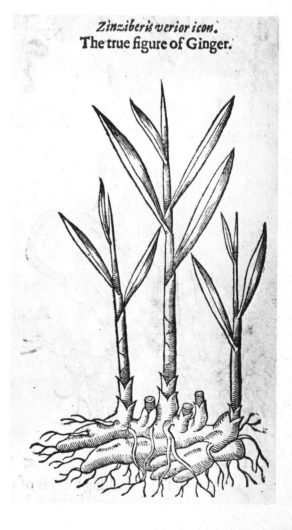

Zinziberis verior icon.
The true figure of Ginger.

The Nutmeg

were in the hands of the Portuguese, and del Cano knew that he could expect short shrift if he fell into Dom Manuel's hands. To start with, their voyage was pleasant enough, through the lush and exotic islands of Indonesia. Pigafetta was in his element, chronicling the strange people and stranger creatures they met *en route*:

A little way below Java the Great is an island called Ocoloro. Here there live only women, who become pregnant by the wind. And when they give birth, if the child be male they kill it, and if it be female they rear it. And if any man set foot on this island he is immediately killed. . . . In the land of Cimbombom are certain trees, the leaves of which when they fall to the ground become alive and walk! These leaves are the width of a mulberry leaf but not so long, and at the pointed end are four feet, two on either side. The creatures [*phyllium ortheptara* or stick insects] have no blood, but if anyone touch them they run away. I once kept one for nine days in a cage without food, and when I opened the cage it ran happily this way and that. They cannot, I think, live on anything but air.

Other wonders to intrigue Pigafetta were 'the sandalwood which has to be cut at a certain phase of the moon or else it rots', 'the coral of wondrous hue which looks like a plant but acts like an animal', the 'women of Java who, when their husband dies, fling themselves on his funeral pyre', 'the fish which live happily in trees' and the 'musk which is not properly set till it is steeped in the urine of a cat'.

By the end of March the islands had been left astern, and the *Victoria* was standing into the Indian Ocean with the fair-weather monsoon sweet in her rigging. They made good progress at first, but by the time they reached mid-ocean their provisions had begun to deteriorate. For there had been no salt in Tidor with which they could pickle their chicken and pork, and now, under the heat of the tropic sun, the meat turned putrid. Eventually it had to be jettisoned. The crew were reduced to a diet of water and rice. They became listless and emaciated, and by mid-April were again in the grip of scurvy.

Nor was it only their health that deteriorated; for as spring gave way to summer, the weather also took a turn for the worse. May, in the Indian Ocean, sees the start of the south-west monsoon, a season of high winds, torrential rain and heavy seas. The monsoon seems to have broken early in 1522, and on 16 May the *Victoria* was dismasted in a series of violent storms. The crew, half-starving, soaked to the skin and shivering with cold, begged del Cano to make for Mozambique and hand over

'Their provisions began to deteriorate . . . by mid-April they were again in the grip of scurvy'

his ship to the Portuguese. But the Basque now proved his metal. '*Ma inanti determinamo tutti morir che andar in mano dei Portughesi*', he cried – 'We are determined to die rather than fall into the hands of the Portuguese.' It was as though the iron of Magellan's resolve lived on in the man who now stood in his shoes. The *Victoria* headed still deeper into the Antarctic – as far as forty-two degrees south – and at the end of May she managed at last to limp painfully past the Cape.

Her troubles, however, were far from over. After rounding the Cape of Storms, del Cano had for several weeks the advantage of the Benguela Current and the south-east Trades; but as he neared the Equator both wind and current turned contrary. They made little progress. And soon the twin spectres of famine and scurvy were claiming almost as many victims as they had in the Pacific. Indeed, in some respects the men were worse off now than they had been in the *Mar Pacifico*. There, they had starved from lack of food; now they had food in abundance, only not of the sort that starving men were able to eat – for who on an empty stomach could chew peppercorns, cinnamon or cloves? In the Pacific, also, there had been no known land for them to head for; now they knew very well they were running parallel to the coast of Africa, only they dare not put ashore for fear of the Portuguese. They must that summer have suffered the agony of Tantalus.

When the *Victoria* left Tidor in mid-February there had been sixty men aboard. As she neared the Cape Verdes in early July there were no more than twenty-four. Twenty-seven Europeans and nine Indians had died. 'And when we cast the Christians into the sea,' says the matter-of-fact Pigafetta, 'they sank with their faces upward toward heaven, and the Indians always with their faces down.'

By 8 July the *Victoria* had run out of water as well as of food, and her crew were literally dying on their feet. Del Cano had no option but to make for the Cape Verdes. He landed by night on a lonely beach in Saint Tiago, telling his men to pretend that they had been blown off course from America. The fishermen who met them were sympathetic. It is difficult to say whether or not they realised that their visitors were Spanish, but in any case, bound by the freemasonry of the sea, they took pity on them, and gave them rice and let them fill their casks with water. In the small hours, however, troops arrived from a nearby fort, and del Cano was forced to abandon his landing

'The iron of Magellan's resolve had rubbed off on the man who now stood in his shoes'

Portuguese ships manned by natives were a common sight in the Spice Islands. And, for the final stage of her voyage home the *Victoria*'s now depleted crew, was readily supplemented by native labour.

party – though not before they had ferried aboard several boatloads of supplies – and put hurriedly to sea. It was lucky for him that the next day, 10 July, dawned dull and overcast with banks of mist-cum-cloud drifting low over the sea, and the *Victoria* was able to beat clear of the islands without being sighted.

One thing about their brief visit puzzled Pigafetta, and was to puzzle mathematicians and astronomers for several decades:

When our men went ashore they asked what day it was. They were told that to the Portuguese it was Thursday. Whereat we were much amazed, since to us it was Wednesday, and we knew not how we had fallen into error, especially since the pilot Alvo and I had both written in our log and diary each day without intermission.

An entry which anticipates the need for an international dateline.

The last few weeks of the voyage must have seemed interminable. Indeed if the crew had not been buoyed up by the thought of being so close after so long to their homes, it is doubtful if a single one of them would have survived. For the *Victoria* by now was little more than a floating wreck. Her mainmast was crooked, her mizzen had been carried away, her sails were in shreds and her seams had opened to such an extent that the pumps had to be manned round the clock. While to add to del Cano's troubles there were insufficient seamen to work the ship, so that each man, weak as he was, was obliged to do the work of two or even of three. Sickness and death were their shadows, right up to the final day of their voyage. But at last, on 4 September, they sighted land, 'to us the most blessed headland in all the world', Sagres, the south-westerly tip of Europe.

'Sickness and death were their shadows, right up to the final day of their voyage'

It is impossible to describe how they must have felt, for every one of the nineteen survivors must have despaired many times during the last three years of ever sighting his homeland again.

For forty-eight hours they ran parallel to the coast; then they spotted the Guadalquivir, 'looping through the marshes like a great white snake on its way to couple with the sea'. It was a historic moment, to which Pigafetta's description does scant justice:

In the early morning of Saturday 6 September we entered the bay of San Lucar, and we were only eighteen men, the most part sick.

[Some reports say there were 18 survivors, some 19.] From the time we had departed from San Lucar to the present day we had sailed 14,460 leagues, and completed the circuit of the world from east to west. On Monday 8 September we cast anchor near the Mole of Seville, and discharged our artillery. Next morning we went ashore, barefoot and in our shirts, to the shrine of Our Lady of Victory, each man bearing a lighted candle.

And if this seems a prosaic description with which to bring down the curtain on an epic, the truth is that deeds speak louder than words. In the autumn of 1519 five ships and 277 men had sailed from San Lucar; now, almost exactly three years later, one ship and nineteen men returned. And these men had achieved the *ne plus ultra* of terrestrial exploration: they had circumnavigated the world.

As the survivors made their way that morning through crowded streets to the church of Santa Maria de la Victoria, one can only wish that Magellan had been with them. For without his vision, tenacity and leadership the *Victoria* would never have crossed the Atlantic, let alone the world.

Epilogue

T HERE ARE TWO REASONS why Magellan has seldom been accorded the recognition he merits. Firstly, like King John of England, he suffered from a bad contemporary press. It is easy to see why the Portuguese were displeased with him. Parr sums up their feelings in a single sentence: 'In Portugal the memory of Magellan was excoriated by all writers because of Dom Manuel's hatred of him, and because of the mighty blow he had struck against the Portuguese Oriental Empire.' The displeasure of the Spaniards was due to more complex causes. Magellan had added a great new ocean (the Pacific) and a rich new archipelago (the Philippines) to the Spanish crowns, and one might have expected King Charles to be well pleased with him. Indeed, had Magellan survived the circumnavigation and been able to report to Charles in person, his achievements would very likely have won more recognition. As it was, his exploits were recounted only at second-hand, and then by deserters (Gomes and the crew of the *San Antonio*) and mutineers (del Cano and the crew of the *Victoria*). In order to save their own necks these men, inevitably, did their best to belittle Magellan's achievements and blacken his character. His Strait they described as 'no more than a useless bay': 'We knew', they asserted blandly, 'that it was in the Captain-General's heart to hand over our fleet to the Portuguese.' With Magellan dead and his logs and diaries diplomatically destroyed, such charges were difficult to refute. Only one man, Pigafetta, seems to have had the courage to try to stand up for Magellan, and his support was made largely ineffective by the fact that his diary was expurgated by order of the *Casa de Antillas*.

It was, in fact, the *Casa de Antillas* who were Magellan's most vociferous detractors. In the summer of 1519 the Council had packed Magellan's fleet with its supporters – sons, natural sons, nephews, cousins and friends, all members of the closeknit aristocracy of Andalusia and Castile. Now, three years later, every one of them was dead – and some by Magellan's hand. It must have seemed intolerable to the *Casa de Antillas* that a Portuguese commoner should have dared to lop off the heads of the nobility of Spain. To them he was an ogre, 'spawned by the devil, witness his cloven hoof'; and no calumny regarding his motives or character was too preposterous to be disseminated as fact.

One thing might have salvaged Magellan's reputation. In the eyes of the world wealth and the expectation of wealth have often been looked on as a propitiation of sins. If, therefore, the Captain-General had discovered the treasure of the Incas on a quick and easy route to the Spiceries, all might have been forgiven. But he did not. Which brings us to the second reason why Magellan has never been accorded the recognition he deserves: the lands he reached were so distant and the route to them that he pioneered so dangerous that his discoveries brought little commercial reward.

In this Magellan was the antithesis of Columbus. Columbus's *Santa Maria* sailed for some eight thousand miles across a reasonably placid ocean; Magellan's *Victoria* sailed for some forty-two thousand miles through some of the most terrible storm-belts on earth. Of Columbus's voyage some five thousand miles were made through unknown waters; of Magellan's voyage more than twenty-two thousand miles were through 'seas no Christian man as yet had entered into'. But the route which Columbus pioneered opened up a much-used seaway to the New World; in the wake of the *Santa Maria* sailed a whole

Magellan's skilful and
persistent search for a way
round South America was
recognised as an almost
superhuman achievement.
This allegorical engraving
shows him sailing through the
Strait guided by the gods of
sea and sky.

genealogy of vessels – treasure galleons, slavers, traders, sunshine cruises. The route which Magellan pioneered, on the other hand, was seldom used by anyone. For far from turning out to be the quick and safe short cut to the Orient of which he had dreamed, it proved a slow and extremely hazardous long way round. Indeed, in the half-century which followed Magellan's death so many vessels either failed to find his Strait or came to grief in its passage that *el paso* drifted once again into the limbo of mythology. In 1560, for example, it was categorically stated that 'the Strait of Magellan no longer exists; either a landslide has blocked it or else an island has risen out of the sea to dam up its channel'.

Yet, despite its barren results, Magellan's voyage was a momentous achievement, a feat of seamanship that never has been and never will be surpassed. In the fields of cartography and navigation it added enormously to man's knowledge of the world. And, perhaps most important of all, it eliminated uncertainty from a whole range of mathematical and scientific assumptions. For there could, from now on, be no going back to such bizarre conceptions as the Christian Father's non-concentric globe or uninhabited Antipodes: the basic structure of our planet had been for all time unquestionably ascertained.

If what Magellan *did* is obvious, what he *was* is more open to interpretation. Some have depicted him as a self-willed tyrant; others virtually as a saint – a simple seaman dedicated unselfishly to his calling. These different views are not to be wondered at, for great men are nearly always figures of controversy, and greatness is a quality which Magellan undoubtedly possessed. He was a leader: a man of decision; a good friend but a dangerous enemy.

But perhaps the last word on him should be left to someone who was unbiased and who knew him intimately, the matter-of-fact and level-headed Pigafetta:

Magellan's main virtues were courage and perseverance, in even the most difficult situations; for example he bore hunger and fatigue better than all the rest of us. He was a magnificent practical seaman, who understood navigation better than all his pilots. The best proof of his genius is that he circumnavigated the world, none having preceded him.

Select Bibliography

The basic source for all books on Magellan is *Magellan's Voyage, a Narrative Account of the First Circumnavigation* by Antonio Pigafetta. The complete edition has only recently been made available in the English language – translated by R.A.Skelton and published in 1969 by the Yale University Press.

Other biographies include:
Life of Ferdinand Magellan, F.H.H.Guillemard [London, 1890]
Conqueror of the Seas, S.Zweig [New York, 1938]
Fernão de Magalhães, Visconde de Lagôa [Lisbon, 1938]
So Noble a Captain, C. M. Parr [London, 1955]

A major work, which may well prove the definitive biography, is in preparation by Samuel Eliot Morison.

Useful books for background reading include:
Historia da Expensão Portuguesa No Mundo, A.Baião [Lisbon, 1937]
História de España de sus Indies, D.V.Gebhardt [Barcelona, 1864]
Explorers' Maps, R.A.Skelton [London, 1958]
The Ship, Bjorn Landström [London, 1962]
Southward the Caravels, E.Bradford [London, 1961]
The Caravels of Christ, G.Renault [London, 1959]
The Exploration of the Pacific, J.C.Beaglehole [London, 1934]

Acknowledgements

The author and publishers wish to thank those responsible for granting permission to quote extracts from the following publications.

Parr, C. M., *So Noble a Captain*, John Farqueharson Ltd, London, 1955
Pigafetta, Antonio, *Magellan's Voyage*, Yale University Press, London, 1969, translated by R. A. Skelton
Zweig, S., *Magellan: Pioneer of the Pacific*, Cassell & Co. Ltd, London, 1938. This edition was also published in America under the title *Conqueror of the Seas*

List of Illustrations

Map drawn by DESIGN PRACTITIONERS LIMITED

Picture research by CAROL GLASS-STORYK

Index